The Moral Basis
of a Backward Society

In such condition, there is no place for industry; because the fruit thereof is uncertain: and consequently
no culture of the earth; no navigation, nor use of the
commodities that may be imported by sea; no commodious building; no instruments of moving, and
removing, such things as require much force; no
knowledge of the face of the earth; no account of
time; no arts; no letters; no society; and which is
worst of all, continual fear, and danger of violent
death; and the life of man, solitary, poor, nasty,
brutish, and short.

—Hobbes

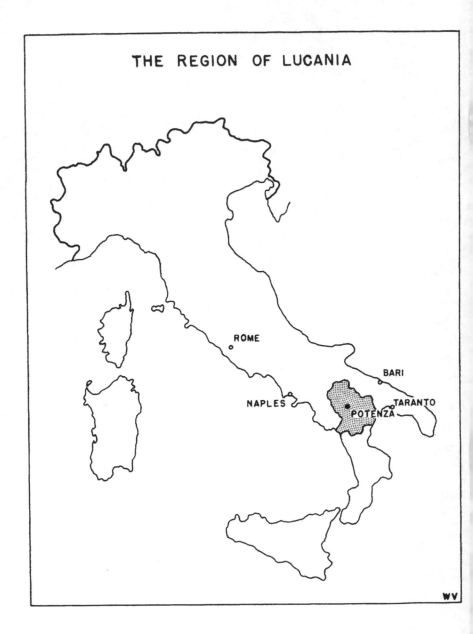

THE REGION OF LUCANIA

ROME

BARI

NAPLES   TARANTO
           POTENZA

WV

The Moral Basis of a Backward Society

EDWARD C. BANFIELD

With the assistance of Laura Fasano Banfield

PHOTOGRAPHS BY THE AUTHOR

THE FREE PRESS

NEW YORK   LONDON   TORONTO   SYDNEY   TOKYO   SINGAPORE

THE FREE PRESS
A Division of Simon & Schuster Inc.
1230 Avenue of the Americas
New York, NY 10020

THE FREE PRESS and colophon are trademarks
of Simon & Schuster Inc.

Manufactured in the United States of America

20   19   18   17   16   15

Library of Congress Catalog Card Number: 58-9398

ISBN Number: 0-02-901510-3

FIRST FREE PRESS PAPERBACK EDITION 1967

Contents

Introduction

In democratic countries the science of association
is the mother of science; the progress of all the rest
depends upon the progress it has made.

—Tocqueville

Most of the people of the world live and die without ever
achieving membership in a community larger than the family
or tribe. Except in Europe and America, the concerting of
behavior in political associations and corporate organization is a
rare and recent thing.

Lack of such association is a very important limiting factor in
the way of economic development in most of the world. Except as people can create and maintain corporate organization,
they cannot have a modern economy. To put the matter positively: the higher the level of living to be attained, the greater
the need for organization. Inability to maintain organization is
also a barrier to political progress. Successful self-government
depends, among other things, upon the possibility of concerting
the behavior of large numbers of people in matters of public concern. The same factors that stand in the way of effective association for economic ends stand in the way of
association for political ones too. "The most democratic country on the face of the earth," Tocqueville observed, "is that in
which men have, in our time, carried to the highest perfection

7

the art of pursuing in common the object of their common desires and have applied this new science to the greatest number of purposes." [1]

We are apt to take it for granted that economic and political associations will quickly arise wherever technical conditions and natural resources permit. If the state of the technical arts is such that large gains are possible by concerting the activity of many people, capital and organizing skill will appear from somewhere, and organizations will spring up and grow. This is the comfortable assumption that is often made.

The assumption is wrong because it overlooks the crucial importance of culture. People live and think in very different ways, and some of these ways are radically inconsistent with the requirements of formal organization. One could not, for example, create a powerful organization in a place where everyone could satisfy his aspirations by reaching out his hand to the nearest coconut. Nor could one create a powerful organization in a place where no one would accept orders or direction.

There is some reason to doubt that the non-Western cultures of the world will prove capable of creating and maintaining the high degree of organization without which a modern economy and a democratic political order are impossible. There seems to be only one important culture—the Japanese—which is both radically different from our own and capable of maintaining the necessary degree of organization. If there is to be more than a superficial overlay of industrialization in China, India, and the other underdeveloped countries, their ethos must be such as to allow the establishment of corporate forms of action.

The ability of a culture to maintain organization cannot meaningfully be measured simply in number or size of organizations. An organization may have many members and cover a large area and yet do very little. In appraising the capacity of a culture to maintain organization, it is necessary to consider not only numbers and size of organizations but their efficiency, i.e., the rate at which they convert valued input to valued output. In doing this, one must ask how exacting are the purposes or

1. *Democracy in America*, Knopf edition, Vol. II, p. 107.

values being served: obviously it is less of a feat to be efficient in the attainment of a purpose which imposes few demands than in the attainment of one which imposes many. That a culture is able to maintain an effective military force, for example, does not imply that it can succeed in the infinitely more difficult task of creating an industrial society in which human values are preserved and improved. If these most difficult and important purposes are taken as the standard, it is even more difficult to see how most cultures of the non-Western world can attain a high level of organization unless they are changed drastically or potentialities now latent in them find expression.

While it is easy to see that culture may be the limiting factor which determines the amount and character of organization and therefore of progress in the less developed parts of the world, it is not obvious what are the precise incompatibilities between particular cultures, or aspects of culture, and particular forms or levels of organization. Even with respect to our own society we know very little about such matters. What, for example, is the significance for organization of various class, ethnic, or sexual attributes within our own culture?

This book is a study of the cultural, psychological, and moral conditions of political and other organization. The approach is that of detailed examination of factors which impede corporate action in a culture which, although not radically foreign to ours, is nevertheless different from it and in some respects closely similar to that of the Mediterranean and Levantine worlds.

The book is about a single village in southern Italy, the extreme poverty and backwardness of which is to be explained [2] largely (but not entirely) by the inability of the

2. An explanation, someone has said, is a place where the mind comes to rest. Some of the explanations discussed (Chapter Two) or offered (Chapter Eight) in this book are causal, i.e., they are places where the mind comes to rest when it looks for conditions antecedent to an event and necessary to its occurrence. Others (Chapter Five) are at least superficially of a different sort: they are places where the mind comes to rest when it looks for a principle of identity in seemingly unrelated facts.

villagers to act together for their common good or, indeed, for any end transcending the immediate, material interest of the nuclear family. This inability to concert activity beyond the immediate family arises from an ethos [3]—that of "amoral familism"—which has been produced by three factors acting in combination: a high death rate, certain land tenure conditions, and the absence of the institution of the extended family.

Our family—my wife and I and our two children, then eight and ten years old—lived among the peasants of Montegrano (the name is fictitious, as are all local ones) for nine months in 1954 and 1955. With the help of an Italian student, my wife interviewed about 70 persons, most of them peasants. (My own knowledge of the language was non-existent to start with and rudimentary later.) In addition, we gathered data from census schedules and other official sources, from record books and autobiographies kept by peasants at our request, and from thematic apperception tests.

It was not practical to employ sophisticated sampling techniques. (To have done so would have left no time for interviewing.) Therefore, we do not know how representative our interviews were; our impression is, however, that they were highly representative of that part of the population which lives in the town and reasonably representative of the nearby country dwellers. We are not competent to say how representative Montegrano is of southern Italy as a whole; there is some evidence, however, that in the respects relevant to this study, Montegrano is fairly the "typical" south, viz., the rest of Lucania, the regions of Abruzzi and Calabria, the interior of Campania, and the coasts of Catania, Messina, Palermo, and Trapani.[4]

3. The concept "ethos" is used in Sumner's sense: "the sum of the characteristic usages, ideas, standards, and codes by which a group is differentiated and individualized in character from other groups." *Folkways*, p. 36.

4. An Australian demographer, J. S. McDonald, has shown that emigration rates in these areas "where economic aspirations were integrated only with the welfare of the individual's nuclear family" have been higher than in other rural districts (i.e., the Veneto, Centre, Emilia-Romagna, Tus-

Since our intention is not to "prove" anything, but rather to outline and illustrate a theory which may be rigorously tested by any who care to do so, we think our data—meager though they are—are sufficient. There are enough data, at least, to justify systematic inquiry along these lines. Until such inquiry has been made, the argument made here must be regarded as highly tentative.

Some readers may feel that amoral familism, or something very much akin to it, exists in every society, the American no less than the southern Italian. Our answer to this is that amoral familism is a pattern or syndrome; a society exhibiting *some* of the constituent elements of the syndrome is decisively different from one exhibiting *all* of them together. Moreover, the matter is one of degree: no matter how selfish or unscrupulous most of its members may be, a society is not amorally individualistic (or familistic) if there is somewhere in it a significant element of public spiritedness or even of "enlightened" self interest.

We wish to express appreciation for the interest and courtesies extended by Professor Manlio Rossi-Doria and Dr. Gilberto Marselli of the *Scuola Agraria* in Portici and to Drs. Giuseppe Barbero and Giuseppe Orlando of the *Istituto Nazionale di Economia Agraria* in Rome. Mr. Giovanni Giura, now of Chicago, assisted in the field work in Montegrano. Dr. Ivano Rinaldi of Perugia administered thematic apperception tests in the Rovigo district and supplied information on social organization there.

Acknowledgment is due the Social Science Division of the University of Chicago, which financed the study with funds from the Ford Foundation, and the Social Science Research Council, which also made a grant-in-aid.

Acknowledgment is made to Farrar, Straus, and Cudahy,

---

cany, Umbria, and Marches) "where aspirations for material betterment were expressed in board associative behavior." "Italy's Rural Social Structure and Emigration," *Occidente*, Vol. XII, No. 5 (September–October 1956), pp. 437–455.

Inc., publishers of Carlo Levi's *Christ Stopped at Eboli*, for permission to quote from that book, and to Donald S. Pitkin for permission to quote from his doctoral dissertation, *Land Tenure and Family Organization in an Italian Village*.

The present tense describes the situation as it was in 1955.

The Moral Basis
of a Backward Society

1

Impressions and Questions

AMERICANS are used to a buzz of activity having as its purpose, at least in part, the advancement of community welfare. For example, a single issue of the weekly newspaper published in St. George, Utah (population 4,562), reports a variety of public-spirited undertakings. The Red Cross is conducting a membership drive. The Business and Professional Women's Club is raising funds to build an additional dormitory for the local junior college by putting on a circus in which the members will be both clowns and "animals." The Future Farmers of America (whose purpose is "to develop agricultural leadership, cooperation, and citizenship through individual and group leadership") are holding a father-son banquet. A local business firm has given an encyclopedia to the school district. The Chamber of Commerce is discussing the feasibility of building an all-weather road between two nearby towns. "Skywatch" volunteers are being signed up. A local church has collected $1,393.11 in pennies for a children's hospital 350 miles away. The County Farm Bureau is flying one of its members to Washington, 2,000 miles away, to participate in discussions of farm policy. Meetings of the Parent Teachers Associations are being held in the schools. "As a responsible citizen of our community," the notice says, "you belong in the PTA."

Montegrano, a commune of 3,400 persons, most of them poor farmers and laborers, in the province of Potenza in southern

Italy,[1] presents a striking contrast. The commune consists of a town, lying like a white beehive against the top of a mountain, and twenty-seven square miles of surrounding fields and forests. One-third of the Montegranesi live on scattered farms at the base of the mountain and in the valley around it. The others live in the town, but since they are mostly farmers and laborers, their waking hours are spent in the fields below the town or on the footpaths that wind between town and country.

No newspaper is published in Montegrano or in any of the thirteen other towns lying within view on nearby hilltops. Occasional announcements of public interest—"there are fish for sale in the *piazza* at 100 *lire* per *chilo*"—are carried by a town crier wearing an official cap, who toots a brass horn to attract attention. Official notices are posted in the salt and tobacco store, a government monopoly, and on a bulletin board in the town hall. Several copies of three or four newspapers published in Rome, Naples, and Potenza come into town by bus every day or two, but these of course do not deal much with local affairs and they are read by very few.

Twenty-five upper class men constitute a "circle" and maintain a clubroom where members play cards and chat. Theirs is the only association. None of the members has ever suggested that it concern itself with community affairs or that it undertake a "project."[2]

The merchants of Montegrano are well aware of the impor-

1. Italy is divided into 92 provinces. The province of Potenza includes 97 communes and covers an area of 414 square miles. Its population was 435,495 in 1951. Potenza and Matera provinces together comprise the region of Lucania, or, as it was formerly called, Basilicata.

For a brief, factual account in English of the physical and social geography of southern Italy, see Robert E. Dickinson, *The Population Problem of Southern Italy*, Syracuse University Press, 1955.

2. According to J. S. McDonald (in a personal communication), Calabrian towns over 2,000 population generally have a "circle of nobles" or "circle of gentlemen" (*circulo dei civili*) and sometimes a "circle of workingmen," but "they function only as rendezvous. However, backstreet drinking dens are important: here the local criminals meet. Otherwise there is no continuous membership of a recreation group (outside nuclear family-clique) for the worker-cultivator class."

tance to them of good roads. They would not, however, expect to be listened to by the authorities who decide which roads are to be improved. A Montegrano man might write a letter to the provincial authorities in Potenza or to the newspaper there, but it is unlikely that his doing so would make any difference. In fact, the officials would be likely to resent what they would consider interference in their affairs.

There are no organized voluntary charities in Montegrano. An order of nuns struggles to maintain an orphanage for little girls in the remains of an ancient monastery, but this is not a local undertaking. The people of Montegrano contribute nothing to the support of it, although the children come from local families. The monastery is crumbling, but none of the many half-employed stone masons has ever given a day's work to its repair. There is not enough food for the children, but no peasant or landed proprietor has ever given a young pig to the orphanage.

There are two churches in town and two priests, one the son of a Sicilian peasant and the other the son of a prosperous Montegrano merchant. The churches do not carry on charitable or welfare activities, and they play no part at all in the secular life of the community. Even in religious matters their influence is not very extensive. The life of the town goes on very much as usual on Sunday mornings: the artisans are at work on a new building as usual at seven o'clock, the stores are all open, and the country people are on their way down the mountainside with their donkeys. Of the 3,400 people in the commune, not more than 350 hear mass on Sunday. These are mostly women. The few men who go to mass remain standing near the door as if to signify that they are not unduly devout. When the collection plate is passed, many people give nothing and few give more than a half a cent (five or ten *lire*). By tradition the men of Montegrano are anti-clerical. The tradition goes back a century or more to a time when the church had vast holdings in southern Italy and was callous and corrupt. Today it owns only one small farm in Montegrano, and the village priests are both known to be kindly and respectable men. Nevertheless priests in general—so many Montegranesi insist—are money-grubbers, hypocrites, and worse.

When members of the upper class are asked who is known as particularly public-spirited—what private persons are apt to take the initiative in dealing with matters which involve the public welfare—a few mention the Baron di Longo and Colonel Pienso, both of whom live in Rome and are believed to have great influence there. Most people, however, say that no one in Montegrano is particularly public-spirited, and some find the idea of public-spiritedness unintelligible. When an interviewer explained to a young teacher that a "public-spirited" person is one who acts for the welfare of the whole community rather than for himself alone, the teacher said:

> No one in town is animated by a desire to do good for all of the population. Even if sometimes there is someone apparently animated by this desire, in reality he is interested in his own welfare and he does his own business.
>
> Even the saints, for all their humility, looked after themselves. And men, after all, are only made of flesh and spirit.

Another teacher said that not only is public-spiritedness lacking, but many people positively want to prevent others from getting ahead.

> Truly, I have found no one who interests himself in the general welfare. On the contrary, I know there is tremendous envy of either money or intelligence.

In some southern Italian towns the gentry are said to be indifferent to the misery of the peasants and consumed with hatred for each other. This is not the case in Montegrano. The leading families there get along well together, and many upper class people view the peasant's plight with evident sympathy. These people are not led by their sympathy to try to change things, however.

✓   ✓   ✓

The affairs of the commune are conducted by a mayor and elected council and by the provincial civil service which is

headed by a prefect in Potenza. The mayor and council pro-
pose, but it is the prefect who disposes. Even to buy an ashtray
for the city hall requires approval from Potenza; ordinarily,
after a certain amount of delay, the decisions of the local
elected officials are approved, but this is not always the case
and, of course, approval can never be counted upon.

The prefect is represented in Montegrano by the secretary
of the commune, a career civil servant assigned from Potenza.
With the assistance of two clerks, the secretary transacts all of
the routine business of the town. This includes especially the
maintenance of tax records, of vital statistics, and the making
of disbursements on order of the higher authorities.

The mayor is elected for a four-year term and receives no
salary. He represents the commune on all official occasions,
supervises the municipal officers, is the legal representative of
the commune in dealings with third parties, and has certain
powers of certification. In practice, the elected council has
little power. In fact, it is seldom possible to get a quorum of its
members together at the mayor's call.

The elected officials are office-workers, artisans, and prosperous farmers rather than persons of the highest status. The
mayor, for example, is a retired non-commissioned army officer
and petty landowner. His council includes as deputy mayor a
retired non-commissioned officer in the *carabinieri* police, four
artisans or storekeepers, five office-workers, five teachers, two
farmers, and a lawyer. The lawyer is the only one who is
an "upper-upper," and even he is not of the very highest status.

The officials of the commune have nothing to do with the
schools. A director of schools, independently responsible to
Potenza, resides in Montegrano and has jurisdiction over the
elementary schools of several communes. Public works, another
important function, is also administered altogether apart from
the elected local government.

The police (*carabinieri*) also are under a separate authority,
the Ministry of Justice in Rome. The officer in charge locally
(the "*maresciallo*") cooperates closely with the local authorities, but he is in no sense "their man." As a matter of policy, he

is not a native of the town to which he is assigned, and he and his men are under instructions not to fraternize much with the townspeople. The attitude of the *carabinieri* towards all classes is generally good-tempered, businesslike, and aloof.

✓ ✓ ✓

Although the constitution of Italy guarantees that every child will receive schooling through the age of 14, in Montegrano, as in many other places in Italy, only five grades of school are taught. Unless his family can afford to send him away to school, the Montegrano child normally completes his education at the age of 11 or 12.

One-third of the men and two-thirds of the women who were 21 years of age or over in 1954 had attended less than five grades of school. Only five percent of the men and less than two percent of the women had attended more than five grades.[3]

Children attend school four hours each morning six days a week from the middle of September until the middle of June. Schools are poorly equipped, teachers are poorly paid, and the pupil's and sometimes even the teacher's attendance is irregular. After finishing the fifth grade some pupils can barely read and write or do simple sums. A few years after leaving school, peasant children have often completely forgotten what little they learned. According to a Montegrano school official, one-third of the graduates are illiterate several years after graduation. For the most part these are women. Since 1948, however, a night school for adults has been attended by 12 men a year. Thus in eight years 96 men—two thirds of them farmers or laborers and the other artisans—had learned, or re-learned, to read and write.

Until recently a large proportion of the children living on outlying farms were unable to go to school at all. Country schools have been built, and their hours adjusted to the convenience of the farm people (in some country schools classes

3. Details will be found in Appendix A, Tables 1 and 2.

begin at 6 A.M. and end at 10 A.M.). Few children nowadays are prevented from going to school by distance.

Nevertheless, there are many who do not attend regularly. The school authorities, the priests, and the police make joint efforts to persuade parents to send their children to school, and, if all else fails, a parent may be fined if his child is a chronic truant. Some of the farm people, perhaps because they see no use in five grades of schooling when there is no opportunity for more, send their children to school willingly only so long as they are too young to work in the fields.

Both because the schools are poor and irregularly attended and because during the war the operation of the school system was badly disrupted, nearly 30 percent of those 10–40 years of age were illiterate in 1951. The rate of illiteracy was highest (44%) among farm people living on outlying farms.

An artisan's child who completes five grades of school is usually apprenticed. However, if he is to become more than a third- or fourth-rate craftsman in one of the traditional crafts (tailoring, barbering, carpentry, stone masonry, and black-smithing) he must either go to a newly established trade school in a nearby town or serve an apprenticeship in one of the big cities. If he goes away he may learn to be an automobile mechanic, a welder, a typewriter repairer or the like—skills which would enable him eventually to migrate to the north. But this possibility is not within the reach of many; there are very few artisans who can support their children away from home. Even at the government-run vocational school it is necessary to pay board. And for a Montegrano boy to find a place as an apprentice in a big city is next to impossible unless he has relatives there.

Those few boys and girls who go to "*media*" school (grades 6–8) must also leave town. The nearest *media* is in Basso. Basso is not far away, but the bus schedule does not permit commuting. To go to boarding school is very expensive by Montegrano standards. Boarding schools are run by the urban middle class for the urban middle class: a boy must have a *corredo* of six sheets and pillowcases, two blankets of specified quality, two pairs of "ordinary" and one pair of "dress" shoes, and so on. The *corredo*, a Montegrano mother estimated, costs about $80; other expenses amount to about $25 a month. The curriculum of the *media* emphasizes Latin, French (English is not taught even at the University of Naples), history, literature, and government to the virtual exclusion of scientific and technical subjects. Most of those who go to *media* expect eventually to become teachers, lawyers, government clerks, or physicians.

✓   ✓   ✓

Political parties are of little importance in Montegrano. The Fascists held an occasional rally there to which everyone (except the peasants, most of whom escaped to their fields before dawn) was required to come. Political parties in the usual sense did not exist until after the Second World War, however, and even now they are neither strong nor stable.

The Communist Party, for example, got 157 votes in the last (1956) election, but it has no cell in Montegrano. Its local representative is a tailor who reads *L'Unità*, the Communist daily, but has no other regular connection with the hierarchy. His views are far from orthodox.

We Communists are not really bad people [he explains]. We want only bread and work. We exist because we stand opposed to the injustices of this town. Some people worked full-time building the new town hall. They worked from the day the job began until the day it ended. Others asked for a few days work to earn enough to buy bread and got nothing. This was an injustice. Packages used to come to the town officials from America. Some people always got a share. Others never did. That was an injustice.

America made a big mistake at the end of the war, the Communist tailor thinks. "When America occupied Italy, she should have stayed. It would have been much better for us."

Farmuso, the director of the school district, is a Communist and was once the Communist mayor of another town. He engages in private, informal discussions, but because of his official position does not take a formal part in party affairs in Montegrano. At election times, Communist speakers come from Basso, a larger town where there are paid organizers.

The most influential leader of the extreme left is the physician, Dr. Gino, a Nenni Socialist. Like many doctors in southern Europe, he is a materialist and a socialist by inheritance as well as by training and conviction. (His father is said to have baptized him Franco *Marx* Gino and to have had him dressed for the ceremony in a red rather than a white gown.) Dr. Gino is the owner of one of the few vineyards in Montegrano—only several acres, but enough to make him one of the town's principal proprietors.

As a doctor and as a landed proprietor, Dr. Gino has done favors for many people. He is, moreover, the leading upper-class exponent of an ideology which demands the leveling of class differences and the division of wealth. Consequently he has a certain following or clientele among the peasants and artisans. There are some who feel that if any upper class person has their welfare at heart, it is he. Others owe him for professional services or want to get work at his vineyard. If he saw fit, he could enlarge his following and turn it to political account. He is too proud, however, and too individualistic to subject himself to the inconveniences and annoyances which serious political activity would entail. "There is a lot of falsity in politics," he explains. "You must make more friends than you want and you must act like a friend to many people you don't want to be friendly with. This is so because you must always be thinking of how to build up the party and win friends for it." He would hate the feeling of *having* to attend meetings for the party, and he would hate even more to be reprimanded for saying something out of turn. "I would feel like telling them, 'Go fry an egg.'"

Immediately after the war, in 1945, Dr. Gino overcame his distaste for politics sufficiently to try to organize a branch of the Socialist Party in Montegrano. About one hundred people turned out in the *piazza* at his call and voted to join the party. But when the application forms arrived and it was realized that a few *lire* in dues would be required, all interest died. Dr. Gino paid out of his own pocket for the memberships that had been applied for and never tried to organize anything again. "I was trying to get the workers together and to get a labor union started . . . or at least a group that could act to get what it wanted. But there is no spirit. There is no feeling of working together," he said afterward.

If the presence of a patron like Dr. Gino tends to call a clientele into existence, the presence of a potential clientele also tends to call a patron into existence. Just as some of the Roosevelt family have always found it advantageous to be on the Democratic side, so at least one professional man in every southern Italian town finds satisfaction in taking the part of the workers. A man who would have to compete with many others to make himself influential as a Christian Democrat may have the field to himself as a left-wing socialist.

The strongest party in Montegrano is the Christian Democratic (DC) party—"the party of the priests," as the peasants say. The Montegrano priests are in fact extremely active politically both in the pulpit and out. (One of them even became involved in a fist-fight at an election-eve rally.) Other leading figures include the lawyer, an amiable young man who is one of the most thoughtful people in town, and two retired petty officers of the army and the *carabinieri*, respectively, who are mayor and vice-mayor. In view of widespread anti-clericalism, there is reason to suppose that many voters support the Christian Democratic party despite its connection with the church rather than because of it.

Just before elections the Christian Democratic party distributes small packages of *pasta*, sugar, and clothing to the voters. These are called gifts from the Vatican. The voter would be no less willing to accept gifts from any other quarter. "If the Russians sent over 25 bushels of grain," a defeated candidate remarked after the last election, "the people would vote the Christian Democrats out of office tomorrow."

The Monarchist Party is the only right-wing group of importance. It is supported by the Baron di Longo and other landlord proprietors and by a scattering of individuals in all other social classes. The secretary of the party is a retired petty officer of the *carabinieri* who runs a bar. The Monarchist Party, he says, stands for order, peace, lower taxes, and no revolution. By "order" he means "respect," "not too much criticism," and "giving what is expected in all cases."

A monarchy is the best kind of government because the king is then the owner of the country. Like the owner of a house, when the wiring is wrong, he fixes it. He looks after his people like a father. If you have a child, always you love him more and do more for him than you would for others. It is in this way that the king looks after his people. He wants them to love him. He loves them. In a republic, the country is like a house that is rented. If the lights go out, well, that's all right . . . it's not his house. If the wall chips, well, it's not his house. The renter does not fix it. So with the men who govern a republic. They are not interested in fixing things. If something is not quite right and if they are turned out for it, well, meanwhile they have filled their pocketbooks.

The moderate socialist party (PSDI) has little strength in Montegrano.

The so-called neo-fascist party (MSI) is of no importance.

In Montegrano it is not unusual for party officials to change their allegiances suddenly. Six months after he had made the statement quoted above, the secretary of the Monarchist Party announced that he had become a Communist. A few weeks later he was a Monarchist again.

The variability in the voters' behavior is also striking. There are eleven towns in the election district of which Montegrano is a part. Some are poorer than others, and in some land ownership is more widely diffused than in others. To the casual eye, however, these differences do not seem crucial—all of the towns have in common extreme poverty and isolation. The voting behavior of the towns differs greatly, however. As the following table shows, the Communist vote in them in 1953 ranged from two to forty-six percent and from two to seventy-nine percent in 1956.

Table 1—Percentage of Votes Cast for Parties of Left, Center, and Right, Provincial Elections of 1953 and 1956, Election District which Includes Montegrano

| | | Percentage Voting for | | | | | |
| | | LEFT | | CENTER | | RIGHT | |
Town	Population	1953	1956	1953	1956	1953	1956
Montegrano	3,400	23	18	44	62	33	20
Addo	1,039	46	9	28	72	26	19
Basso	6,473	45	36	46	62	9	2
C	1,169	26	12	57	35	17	53
D	1,100	25	25	55	70	20	5
E	894	22	26	52	49	26	25
F	1,695	19	79	68	17	13	4
G	859	16	21	43	69	41	10
H	2,064	8	2	83	68	9	30
I	2,196	7	3	80	73	13	24
J	2,431	2	5	94	89	4	6

Note: "Left" includes Communist and Nenni Socialist parties; "center" Christian Democrat and Saragat Socialist; and "right" Monarchist and MSI.

Variability in voting behavior exists not only from town to town but from election to election within the same town. For example, Addo, the town with the largest percentage of Communist votes in 1953, was solidly Christian Democrat before the 1953 election and again in 1956. But at the same time, town "F" swung violently from the center to the left. Such sudden shifts are not rare in southern Italy.

⸾   ⸾   ⸾

In Montegrano and nearby towns an official is hardly elected before the voters turn violently against him. As soon as he gets into office, his supporters say—often with much justice—he becomes arrogant, self-serving, and corrupt. At the next election, or sooner if possible, they will see that he gets what is coming to him. In Montegrano there is no better way to lose friends than to be elected to office.

In the following letter, written by a lower class Montegranese to a friend abroad, the village political style appears in its characteristic form:

It is true that the Mayor, Vincenzo Spomo, has resigned. That was nearly two months ago. But it was not by his own wish; it was at the prompting of the Council.

As you know, the Council had two factions. Among the Christian Democrats, that is, there were two factions with different ideas, factions which had never agreed from the beginning. Spomo, always in character, wanted to command things for his own purposes. He thought it was as it used to be in the old administration, but this time he had to deal with people who were college graduates . . . who really had some brains. It was not as he thought.

Every now and then the Council met. When he brought up something the members did not like, they would oppose him once, twice, three times, until he was beaten. But one night at a Council meeting he was forced to resign.

Now I want to tell you a little about Spomo. The people were always unhappy with him. He pleased himself. He helped only those he wished to help. All the circulars that came he locked up in his drawer and would not even inform the Council members of them. It was not so much his own will as that of his followers that carried him along, and if the Christian Democrats lost votes it was on account of him personally.

As I said, the Council was divided in two factions. Seven were in favor of Spomo and eleven were in favor of the present mayor. When Spomo heard how the voting went and that he was beaten, he got up without saying a word to anyone and left. Naturally, the new mayor got to his feet and began to thank all those who had voted for him, and the crowd applauded him and acclaimed him until he had to stay the applause with his hands . . . so long did the applause last.

The people are happier because this new mayor is on the side of everyone, listens to everyone, answers everyone, and wants the mass of the workers to be protected.

We will wait and see.

You know what I think about it? I am glad that Spomo no longer governs. He ended up by commanding with the haughtiness of a marshal of the army, just as if he were commanding his soldiers. It was the way he thought—that he was commanding the people of Montegrano. Those he liked he would raise to the stars and those he did not like he would crush. His tongue was for nothing but scolding, and he believed himself a superman. He gave the impression that we were living in the era of the feudal lords.

As for the people, what they think depends upon who they are. If they received favors, they are followers. Those who received neither good nor evil from him, they just repeat what they hear. The majority of those who talk are peasants and laborers.

One morning a jitney driver and a peasant were in the bar. The driver said that one could not find the equal of Spomo as the head of the administration for this town. The other said, "Perhaps so when it came to presumption and promises, but when it came to something positive, the mayor had nothing." Then the driver said that besides being good and fine the mayor had a lot of support—"the support of many influentials, especially the Minister of Agriculture, the prefect, and others. If the Mayor falls [this was before he did fall], the prefect will send a commissioner and the town will see that it will have to pay $5.00 a day [for the support of the commissioner] and in the end Spomo, who is the secretary of the Christian Democratic party, will be appointed commissioner . . . so you will see that he will be not only mayor but also commissioner and you will have to pay him."

The peasant answered that in any event we will pay less than the vacations he has had and the waste he has made have cost during his administration. The argument came very short of ending in blows.

I don't even mention the dissatisfaction of Nino's peasants who had been promised electricity in their zone and heard nothing about it since. Now they don't want to hear or know anything about it. They say that at the next elections they are not going to vote for anyone at all because they [the politicians] are all in it for themselves only.

Of this new mayor one can say nothing as yet because he has not been in very long. I can say only one thing with accuracy—that so persistent were Councilmen Viva and Lasso that we have been given—and it has already got underway—a winter work project which will last two months and employ forty workers a day. They will repair the roads and walls of the town.

As regards the gentry, naturally one knows nothing. Or, to say it better, they are reserved and don't let you hear anything.

✓   ✓   ✓

These impressions of political behavior in Montegrano raise a number of questions.

What accounts for the absence of organized action in the face of pressing local problems? Why, for example, is nothing done about the schools? To the peasants, many of whom are desperately anxious for their children to get ahead, the lack of educational opportunity is one of the bitterest facts of life. Upper class people are affected too; some of them would like to live in Montegrano and cannot do so because it would cost too much to send their children away to a boarding school. One might think, then, that improvement of the local school would be an important local issue—one on which people would unite in political parties or otherwise. Failing to persuade the government to build a *media* school, upper class volunteers might teach an additional grade or two. Or, if this is too much to expect, the bus schedule might be changed so that the Montegrano children could commute to nearby Basso for the higher grades. However, such possibilities have not been considered.

The nearest hospital is in Potenza, five hours away by automobile. For years Montegrano people have complained that the state has not built a hospital in the village. The doctor and two or three other people have written letters to Rome urging that one be built, but that is as far as the effort to get one has gone. Candidates for local office do not campaign on the hospital "issue," and there has been no organized effort to bring pressure to bear upon the government. Nor has there been any consideration of stopgap measures such as might be taken locally—for example, equipping an ambulance to carry emergency cases from Montegrano and other nearby towns to Potenza.

These, of course, are only two of many possible examples of needs which would give rise to community action in some countries,[4] but about which nothing is done in Montegrano.

The question of why nothing is done raises other questions.

4. Cf. for example the handling of the school problem in the southern French village described by Laurence Wylie in *Village in the Vaucluse,* Harvard University Press, 1957, pp. 223–227.

Why are the political parties themselves so unconcerned with local issues? Why is there no political "machine" in Montegrano, or even any stable and effective party organization? What explains the marked differences in the appeal of left, center, and right from town to town among towns that on the surface seem so much alike? What explains the erratic behavior of the electorate in a single town from one election to the next? And why do those elected to office at once lose credit with their supporters?

The remainder of this book is a search for answers to these specific questions and, above all, to the general question: what accounts for the political incapacity of the village?

2

Some Usual Explanations

Six answers, each having a strong appeal to common sense, are given in Montegrano and elsewhere in Italy to the questions raised at the end of the last chapter.

1. Most people in Montegrano are desperately poor. Many have nothing to eat but bread, and not enough of that. Even the well-to-do are poor by American standards. Such a town cannot support a newspaper or the kinds of activity which a newspaper would report. The peasant must go to his fields at dawn and he must work there until it is dark. The blacksmith must be at his forge when the peasant passes on his way to his fields. There is no time for political life in a society so poor.

2. The peasant is as ignorant as his donkey and the artisan is hardly less so. One-third of the men and two-thirds of the women of Montegrano cannot read or write. Some peasants have never been beyond the next village, four miles away. People so ignorant can have no notion of what it is possible to accomplish politically and they cannot make meaningful choices among parties and candidates. Indeed, such things do not enter into their world at all. The peasants, Carlo Levi wrote, "were not Fascists, just as they would never have been Conservatives or Socialists, or anything else. Such matters had nothing to do with them; they belonged to another world and they saw no sense in them. What had the peasants to do with

35

Power, Government and the State? The State, whatever form
it might take, meant 'the fellows in Rome.' " [1]

3. Political behavior reflects class interests and antagonisms.
The upper class gives the village no leadership because it lives
by exploiting the peasant and can do so only by keeping him in
poverty and ignorance.[2] The lower class hates the upper and
seeks for revenge upon it. Collaboration between the classes is
impossible, although nothing can be done without it.

4. Workers who have a plot of land, however small, want to
maintain the *status quo*. On the other hand, those who are landless and must depend upon a large employer see that security
is to be had by collective action, the only effective vehicle of
which is the Communist Party. Thus Montegrano peasants,
most of whom have a bit of land, are conservative or politically
indifferent, whereas those of nearby Basso, who are mostly
laborers on large estates, are Communists. Differences in political behavior are to be accounted for by the circumstances of
land tenure.

5. Centuries of oppression have left the peasant with a pathological distrust of the state and all authority. "To the peasants,"
Carlo Levi writes, "the State is more distant than heaven and far
more of a scourge, because it is always against them." [3]

6. The southern Italian is a despairing fatalist. He believes

1. Carlo Levi, *Christ Stopped at Eboli*, Penguin Edition, p. 52.
2. The real enemies of the peasant, according to Carlo Levi, "those
who cut them off from any hope of freedom and a decent existence, are
to be found among the middle-class village tyrants. This class is physically and morally degenerate and no longer able to fill its original function. It lives off petty thievery and the bastardized tradition of feudal
rights. Only with the suppression of this class and the substitution of
something better can the difficulties of the South find a solution." *Op.
cit.*, p. 176.
    It should be remembered that Levi's observations were made during an
exile which began in 1935 and that his book, which was widely read by
the upper class in Montegrano and other southern towns, no doubt produced an effect. At any rate, it was curious in 1955 to find upper class
people quoting him with approval, although with reference not so much
to their own town as to others and to the Fascist period.
3. Levi, *op. cit.*, p. 52.

that the situation is hopeless and that the only sensible course
is to accept patiently and resignedly the catastrophes that are
in store. [4]

These theories have obvious implications for action. If the
political incapacity of the southern town is due to poverty, then
increasing incomes will increase political capacity. If it is due
to ignorance, then increasing the level of education will increase
political capacity. If it is due to a pathological distrust of the
state, then a sufficiently long experience with a welfare state
will overcome that distrust. Similarly, the solution may be, as
Levi advises, the suppression of the upper class and the substitution for it of something better; large-scale undertakings (like
La Cassa per il Mezzogiorno, a government corporation for
resource development in the south) to convince the southerner
that all is not hopeless, or perhaps some combination of these.

There is an element of truth in each of the theories, but none
of them is fully consistent with the facts that have to be taken
into account, and one could not on the basis of any of them—or
of all of them together—predict how the people of Montegrano
would behave in a concrete situation.

The peasant's poverty is appalling to be sure, but it does not
prevent him from contributing a few days of labor now and
then to some community undertaking like repairing the orphanage. In fact, he uses his poverty as an excuse for not doing
what he would not do anyway: he does not go to mass on
Sunday, he explains sadly, because he must be off to his field at
dawn. But his field is a tiny patch of wheat on which, except
for three weeks a year, he can do almost nothing. There is
hardly a man in Montegrano who could not contribute a third
of his time to some community project without a loss of income.

Nor is the peasant's ignorance sufficient to account for his
political incompetence. Of forty-two peasants who were asked
what the Communists *claim* to stand for, only one was without
an opinion. Most of the opinions were reasonable. Twenty-six
persons said that the Communists claim to stand for equality,
and the replies of most of the others—e.g., "peace, liberty, and

4. *Ibid.*, p. 129.

work," "work for all," "opposition to the church," and "taking from the rich"—also showed comprehension. Some were very thoughtful. Here, for example, is Prato's:

> They say they are going to divide the property and give us all a piece. But what are they going to divide in Montegrano? The only land that could be divided is the Baron's. But he has it all in tenant-operated farms now. They are quite large and perhaps they could be divided. But you have to remember that as matters stand each of those farms supports ten families when you consider the year-round and the day-laborers who work for the tenants. Who is to say it would be better if that land were divided? Who is to say that the land would be better cultivated or that more people could live on it?

Most of the peasants warmly approve the ideal of social equality. They are not so simple-minded, however, as to suppose that Communist claims can be taken at face value. Fourteen of those who were asked what the Communists claim to stand for went on to say that their claims had to be distinguished from their real intentions. The Communists, these peasants said, use the equality argument to get themselves into power.

> The Communists would like us all to be equal and so they would install equalization in Italy. In reality, however, it is certain that they don't like us and are probably looking after their own interests and wanting the command.

Certainly the erratic swings of the electorate to and from Communism cannot be explained on the grounds that the peasant has no idea of what is at stake. He has a sufficient idea— as much or more, perhaps, as the working class voter in the United States—and the artisan has an even better idea. "Italy," one of them remarked, "is too poor a country to afford the luxury of Communism."

The history of the American frontier provides numerous examples of people whose poverty and ignorance were as great or greater than that of the Montegranesi, but whose capacity for self-government and mutual aid was nevertheless extraordinarily great. St. George, Utah, for example, which was mentioned in the first paragraph of Chapter One, was a century ago a desert of sand and rock inhabited only by a handful of miserable Indians subsisting on vermin. The resource base of southern Italy, poor as it is, is far better than that which the Mormons found on the site of St. George. In St. George, incidentally, as in many frontier towns, there was a weekly newspaper at a time when the local economy was based on handicrafts and self-sufficing agriculture and most of the population spelled out its letters painfully one by one.

If the Montegrano peasant had a mystical or sentimental attachment to the land or if he "belonged to another world" which he could not see beyond or which he would not leave, he should be compared to the American Indian rather than to the frontiersman. But with few exceptions, he loathes the land, is acutely aware of the larger society about him, and wants desperately to be fully a part of it.

Class antagonism does not explain Montegrano's political behavior either. If it did, one might expect to find the peasants uniting in action *against* the upper class. But there is no such action, nor is there likely to be. Class and status relations do, however, influence the situation profoundly in ways that are diffuse, indirect, and hard to identify. Like poverty and ignorance, they are general conditions which, so to speak, form the causal background.

In Montegrano peasants do not have a pathological distrust of the state. Such distrust as they have is better described as "normal" and "healthy." When they were asked, "What kind of people are in authority today?", they usually said, in effect, "All kinds." Here are some unexceptional replies:

Do you mean people in the Chamber of Deputies? Most of them are Christian Democrats. The Christian Democrats are the better people—they are thoughtful . . . really trying to help. With the others, so long as they are getting theirs they don't care.

ϒ ϒ ϒ

You mean the military, like the generals, and the pope and his cardinals? Some are good and some are bad.

ϒ ϒ ϒ

The chief of the government is Pella. Pella is a good type—intelligent. If he were not intelligent, they would not let him be head of the government. Always it is those who are very intelligent.

Sometimes the peasant thinks of the state as a source of help. Eighteen were asked what they would do if someone owed them $3 or $4 and would not pay. All but five said that they would take the debtor to the Marshal of the *carabinieri*. The others would not go to law, not, however, from pathological distrust of the state, but because they would not want to make enemies.

When they were asked what they would do if someone in the neighborhood hid a person who was sick with a contagious disease, twelve said they would inform the doctor (who is the town health officer). Eight others would do nothing, not, however, from distrust of the state, but because they would not want to "humiliate" the family or act in a way that would be thought unfriendly.[5]

Fourteen peasants (some of them women) were asked, "What would you do if you saw a policeman give a bad beating to someone who had done nothing wrong?" The replies were as follows:

Try to convince him of his error.	(Four)
Report him to the Marshal.	(Three)
Nothing, because before the law one must be quiet.	(Three)
Let him taste some blows.	(Four)

Fear of the authorities is not a specifically peasant attitude; many peasants are not fearful and some who are not peasants are extremely so. The Communist director of schools, among the best educated men in Montegrano, when asked what he would do if he saw a policeman beating an innocent man, said

5. In answer to the question, "What would you do if you knew that someone was contemplating suicide?" most people said they would advise or plead with the person; a few said they would tell his family, and still fewer would call the police or the doctor. No one mentioned the priest.

he would not interfere unless the victim were a friend or relative. The police, he pointed out, might make reprisals against one who interfered.

Many peasants regard the government as a friend: they say it is the only source from which they have ever received help.

The theory that the southern Italian is prevented by melancholy fatalism from taking effective action does not, of course, explain the choices he makes when he *does* act. Nor is it consistent with the fact that when individualistic action is called for he is not incapacitated by despair or fatalism. Many of the peasants of Montegrano, for example, are attempting to limit the size of their families in order to give their children more education and better opportunities for social mobility. This is the behavior of people who believe that it *is* possible to exercise control over the most important matters by taking precautions. There is reason to believe that the southerner's pessimism exists where social rather than individualistic action is called for; he is, then, realistic but not necessarily fatalistic.

Nor do these theories explain voting behavior. It is often said that the Communist vote is heaviest where the pressure of population on resources is greatest (i.e., where chronic poverty is most severe and widespread), where lack of education—and specifically illiteracy—is greatest, and where the proportion of landless laborers to proprietors is greatest. When put to the test in the Montegrano district with such indices as are available, however, these factors do not seem to have any relation to the strength of the Communist vote. As Table 2 shows, illiteracy is highest in the town where the Communist vote was lightest in 1953, population density is not significantly greater where the Communist vote was heavy, and the proportion of laborers is greatest in some of the most conservative towns.

These theories, it should also be noted, do not explain—and may even be inconsistent with—the tendency of voters to shift erratically between right and left from election to election. In the town of Addo, for example, there was a shift from Christian Democratic to Communist and back again to Christian Democratic, although of course there had been no change in

per capita wealth, in literacy, or in the distribution of land
ownership.

Table 2

	Left-Wing[a] Vote (%)	% Illiteracy[b] Among Men	Density of[c] Population	Proportion[d] Laborers (%)
Montegrano	23	31	48	36
Addo	46	37	55	44
Basso	45	31	73	50
C	26	31	49	50
D	25	22	42	31
E	22	31	31	31
F	19	22	47	30
G	16	34	57	66
H	8	37	44	34
I	7	31	45	34
J	2	45	24	64

Notes: (a) Includes Communist and Nenni Socialists, 1953; (b) includes males over six
years old; (c) persons per square kilometer; (d) families the head of which is classified
as a farm laborer as a percentage of all families.

Although they do not in themselves explain Montegrano's
political incapacity, two features of the situation—poverty and
class antagonism—are of such general importance as underlying
conditions that they must be discussed at greater length. This
will be done in the next two chapters. Following that, an alter-
native explanation will be offered.

3

The Economy

MONTEGRANO is as poor as any place in the western world. This fact, although it does not explain the villagers' political incapacity, bears upon it in a very fundamental way.

The land is stony, steep, and poorly watered. It supports light stands of wheat which is planted in November and harvested in June, sparse natural pasture, olive and fig trees, and forests of oak. Here and there a small spring permits irrigation of a fraction of an area on the side of the mountain. Along the banks of the rivers there is also a small amount of irrigated land; but the irregular flow of the rivers—they flood in the spring and trickle in the summer—prevents extensive irrigation. Poor and small as they are, the fields and forests are Montegrano's principal source of income. There is no mining or manufacturing of importance anywhere in the region.

The climate is mild. Average temperatures range from approximately 35 in January and February to approximately 85 in July and August. Rainfall averages 35 inches a year, most of it falling in December and January.

Even by the standards of southern Italy, Montegrano is isolated, a fact which of course helps to make it poor. To the nearest railhead is 40 miles. To the provincial capital, Potenza, it is 90 miles, and from there to Bari on the east coast, it is another 90. All of the highways are narrow, tortuous, and steep. It takes four to five hours to drive to Potenza in a small Italian car.

Busses stop at Montegrano four times a day (twice each way), except on Sundays. They carry mail, newspapers, and a small amount of freight. To Naples by bus takes eight hours and costs $2.75.

There are five automobiles in Montegrano, all of them for hire at from nine to twelve cents a mile, depending on the length of the trip. No one owns a car for private purposes.

The traffic into Montegrano consists of an occasional official on a tour of inspection, an infrequent truckload of merchandise, fertilizer, building materials, cordwood, or potatoes, and now and then a visitor who comes, usually from Potenza, Bari, Naples, or Salerno, to see relatives. Casual tourists never come to Montegrano, and the arrival of a strange car there is an event which attracts general interest.

There is a telegraph in the post office and a public telephone in the town hall; this is the only telephone in town. In 1955 there were radios in two bars and in 40 or 50 homes. A moving picture house with about 100 seats had nightly showings of 16 millimeter Italian and occasional foreign films; the admission was 16 cents for preferred seats and 10 cents for all others. A theatre in which 35 millimeter films could be shown is now under construction, however, and the number of radios increases by several a month.

In the normal course of their lives (that is, leaving war-time experience out of account) most Montegranesi have little or no direct contact with the world beyond their town. Except for the relatively few who will be described as "upper class," most of the townspeople make no use of the highways and other communications facilities. They do not take the bus. They do not read the newspapers. They do not go to the movies. They do not go into the bars to listen to the radio. They send no telegrams, make no telephone calls, and, except on rare occasions, write no letters. Most of them, in fact, can rarely afford to buy postage stamps, and two-thirds are unable, or virtually unable, to read or write.

When the farm people of Montegrano travel, it is on foot leading a donkey to the sides of which large baskets are fixed.

Instead of following the highways which, being built for automobiles, wind endlessly around the mountains to maintain a reasonable grade, the farm people follow trails down the mountain. No one uses a cart; the advantage of the cross-country trails over the highways is too great and, besides, none of the farm people has very much to transport. The range of travel, then, is limited to nearby towns. Many people have never travelled beyond these neighboring towns and some women have never left Montegrano.

Between Montegrano and the nearby places there is a good deal of intermarriage. (In 77 marriages performed in Montegrano in recent years, seven brides and 26 grooms were natives of other towns; all seven of these brides and 15 of the 26 grooms came from towns within easy walking distance; only two grooms came from as far away as Potenza.) Consequently a good many Montegrano people have relatives to visit and property to look after in these other towns.

In the summer each town has two or three one-day fairs in connection with its *festa* or saint's day celebrations. On fair days people come to town from half a dozen nearby places—from as far, in fact, as it is convenient to drive a pig. Gypsies and other livestock dealers, as well as merchants with yard-goods, cooking utensils, and other hardware displayed in trucks, come from much greater distances and go from one fair to another all summer.

✓ ✓ ✓

With the exception of about a score of gypsy families who trade in livestock, the people of Montegrano belong to seven occupational classes.

1. *Laborers.* About one-fourth of the heads of families are laborers who work on farms and, when opportunity affords, on public works projects. With a few exceptions, these families live in town in one- or two-room houses which they own. Half of them own a small amount of land; the average holding is about three acres. Many own donkeys.

2. *Farmers.* A farmer is defined by the Census as one who

gets more than half his income from land which he works as an owner or renter.[1] By this definition (not a very meaningful one in Montegrano, because many people have a tiny patch of land and are "farmers" perforce when they cannot find work for wages), farmers are the largest single occupational class and one which includes nearly half the population.

Three-fourths of the farmers live on outlying farms; the others live in town. Those who live in the country have much larger farms on the average (17 acres as against 5); indeed, it is because their farms are so small that the town-dwelling farmers do not live on them. Although the country-dwelling farmers have larger farms and are more prosperous, the town-dwelling farmers have more amenities in their homes and more schooling.

3. *Artisans.* Montegrano has several tailors, shoemakers, carpenters, blacksmiths, and housebuilders, as well as dressmakers, bakers, electricians, barbers, a chairmaker, a tinker, and a watch repairer. In all, there are 76 families the heads of which are artisans; this is a little less than 10 percent of the population. Most of the artisans are self-employed and very few have apprentices or employees. About two-thirds of them own a small piece of land. In general the artisans have more education and higher standards of living than the farm people.

4. *Merchants.* Several stores sell general merchandise—mainly food (macaroni and spaghetti, bread, cheese, cold meats, and canned goods), clothing, dry goods, and hardware for the farm and the home. In addition, there is an electrical appliance store, two bars, a cloth store, a printing shop, three meat markets, and a movie. Most of the merchants own small plots of land. On the average they are somewhat better off than the artisans. Two merchants are becoming comparatively rich. These are able and

---

1. The census schedule is filled out for the country people by an official. The official may ask the individual whether he wants to be classified as a farmer or as a laborer or he may make the entry according to his own opinion. Whether a family should be considered "farmer" or "laborer" involves in marginal cases a judgment of social rather than economic status (i.e., of position in the deference hierarchy), but it is impossible to say exactly whose judgment is recorded in the schedules.

vigorous men who accumulated some capital during fascism (they had the only licensed stores, a circumstance which later gave them an advantage in the black-market) and who invested shrewdly afterward.

5. *Office workers.* School, tax, and police officials for a district which includes 17 communes are headquartered in Montegrano. Office workers therefore comprise a somewhat larger proportion of the population than would otherwise be the case: 45 families, about five percent of all, are in this class. About one-third of the office workers own land. Many of the others are not natives of the town and do not expect to live out their lives there. Although their social status is much higher, the incomes of the lowest-paid office workers are less than those of the more prosperous farmers, artisans, and merchants.

6. *Professionals.* There are 10 families of professionals—the doctor, the pharmacist, two priests, the lawyer, the director of schools, and four teachers. Most of them own small amounts of land.

7. *Landed proprietors.* Ten persons are classified by the Census as landed proprietors. Some of these own as little as 20 or 30 acres; they are, however, descendants of families which owned large tracts two or three generations ago, and they manage to live fairly well without doing manual labor. Being a landed proprietor is more a matter of social than of economic status.

The largest landowner is the Baron di Longo, a diplomat who comes from Rome from time to time to collect his rents and oversee his affairs. The Baron owns 18 farms which he operates through tenants. The farms total 855 acres, which is 15 percent of all cultivated land in the commune.

*   *   *

Agriculture and forestry are the main sources of income in Montegrano. About 80 percent of the farms are in holdings of less than 15 acres.[2] These subsistence farms produce little or

2. For details of land use and farm sizes, see Appendix A, Tables 3–5.

nothing for sale. There are usually two or three produce ped-
dlers in the Montegrano public square on summer mornings,
but most of these come by donkey from Basso, where the
lower elevation and the larger amount of irrigated land make
commerical production of fruits and vegetables feasible. The
fruits and vegetables grown in Montegrano are used at home
or exchanged with neighbors for the most part.

Despite their number, the subsistence (and less-than-sub-
sistence) farms occupy less cultivated land than do the 93 farms
which are large enough (15 acres or more) to be called commercial.

Farmers follow a simple crop rotation plan inherited from
antiquity: they plant half their land to wheat each year, following the wheat with a legume which they harvest for forage.
Thus a subsistence farm of, say, 12 acres includes six acres of
wheat from which the normal yield is 7–10 bushels to the acre.[3]
Many feel that they cannot afford to use chemical fertilizers;
others use small amounts. The typical subsistence farm has
several fig trees, enough to give the family an ample supply of
fresh and dried figs. If the lay of the land affords sufficient
shelter, there are also a few olive trees. These bear every other
year. There are usually some sizeable oak trees on the farm.
The farmer trims off the lower branches and feeds the leaves
to oxen or goats, and his wife and children carry home the
branchwood for fuel and gather the acorns for the family pig.
If the farmer is fortunate, he may be able to irrigate a small
plot from a spring. In this case he grows vegetables for family
use, especially peppers, beans, onions, tomatoes (these can sometimes be grown on dry land as well), corn, and greens.

Most of the cultivated land is plowed to a depth of six inches
with a steel-tipped plow drawn by oxen, but if the farmer has
a very small plot and cannot find work for wages, he may save
expenses by using his (and his family's) idle time to break the
ground with mattocks. Grain is harvested by hand with a

3. In the years when there is about three inches of rainfall, the average
in North Dakota is 12 bushels to the acre; when there is more rain, the
average goes as high as 25.

sickle; the land is too rough and farm units are too small to make the use of combines feasible. Some grain is still threshed under the feet of oxen and separated from the chaff by being tossed into the air, but nowadays most farmers carry their grain to a nearby machine where it is threshed at so much per bushel.

In a normal year the value of the production from such a subsistence farm is about $325.[4]

Such a farm is not likely to be all in one piece; it may be in three or four pieces scattered at various elevations on the mountain and even at opposite sides of it. Although it is a time-consuming and tiring task to walk from one field to another, most farmers prefer to have their land in at least two pieces as insurance against crop failure; the hailstorm which strikes one side of the mountain will leave the other untouched. Besides, unless his land is in two pieces, the farmer may not be able to have any that is irrigated. These advantages by no means justify so widespread a division of the land into small scattered parcels; most of the division has resulted from the exigencies of the law of inheritance and, as the farmer sees it, is a necessary evil.

The commercial farms—i.e., the farms of more than 12 acres —produce a little olive oil and wine for sale in local markets. Most of them have some goats or sheep; only one has dairy cattle. All have a few hens or turkeys, but none is specialized in poultry production. Almost without exception, the commercial farmers use chemical fertilizers and follow the two-year rotation of wheat and legumes.

Because manual labor is degrading, a landowner who can do so without starving hires someone to do his work for him. Thus, in general, any farm large enough to produce for the market is worked by a hired laborer (*salariato*) or by a sharecropper (*mezzadro*). The sharecropping arrangement is by far the more common. The owner and the sharecropper agree on what is to be grown and in general how the farm is to be managed. The sharecropper does the day-to-day managing and supplies all of the labor and half of the fertilizer, seed, livestock, and equip-

4. Assuming 64 bushels of wheat at $3.50 per bushel ($225) and valuing the remaining production at $100.

ment. The produce of the farm—except for the kitchen garden, which is usually reserved for the owner—is divided equally. Usually the sharecropper has a written two-year contract. If the farm is large, he may be better off than he would be as the owner of a subsistence plot. Often, however, farms which are large enough to support one family are shared; in such cases the owner's half of the product usually supplements income from other sources, but the sharecropper's half is his whole income, of course.

With the exception of certain government agencies which make loans to farmers (but only to farmers having seven and one-half acres or more!) for the purchase of fertilizer and other supplies, there are no commercial credit sources. The nearest bank (a branch of the Bank of Naples) is in Basso, but it does no business in Montegrano. The merchants will give six months credit at 10 percent for fertilizer. Two or three prosperous individuals occasionally make loans of less than $100 to farmers; these are made out of "friendship" to favored customers. The usual interest rate is two and one-half percent, the amount paid on postal savings, and no collateral is taken.

ᕗ   ᕗ   ᕗ

Carlo Prato, a farm laborer who kept day-to-day records of family income and expenditures in 1955, is an upper-income laborer.[5] He owns two and one-half acres of very poor, hilly land from which he gets 10 bushels of wheat. In addition, he rents an irrigated garden patch which yields a five-month supply of beans, peppers, tomatoes, and greens for family use. This is the average land-holding of those laborers who have land. Nearly half the laborers have no land at all, however. The Pratos own a donkey and a pig, as do eight out of ten laborer families. They are at that stage of the family age cycle—Prato is 43, his wife 36, their daughter, Maria, 16, and their son Peppino, 14—when none of them is too old or too young to work and their family income is therefore higher than it has been or is likely to remain.

5. These records are summarized in Appendix A, Tables 6–7.

Prato was employed 180 days during the year and earned $114 in cash and $90 in kind, mostly meals on the job. This was 60 percent of the family's total earnings. Signora Prato worked very little, partly because her health was poor and partly because there was little opportunity for her to work. The boy was employed occasionally as a stonemason's helper, a job which paid 65 cents a day without meals. Maria, the daughter, worked as a housemaid when she could. The going rate for that kind of work was 33 cents and three meals for a 10- to 12-hour day.[6]

Prato seldom knew a week ahead whether he would find work. On the whole he was lucky. In December and January he was one of the olive oil pressing crew for a big landowner in a nearby town. He lived in a barracks and worked from two in the morning until nine at night for three meals, 25 cents in cash, and half a liter (35 cents worth) of oil a day. When this job ended he was unemployed for a while. Then his turn came on the public employment list and he worked on a road gang. This paid one dollar and one meal for a seven-hour day, but there was a three-hour walk to work and a two-hour walk returning (it was down hill on the way back). At the end of June and during July, the season of the wheat harvest, he found work at good wages—a dollar a day plus three substantial meals —with various landowners of Montegrano. The following three months he was practically unemployed, and he spent his time puttering around his tiny plot of land.

If he could, Prato would have worked for wages every day except *festa* days. So would Maria and Peppino. Signora Prato, despite her poor health, could easily have done all that was essential at home and on their small farm. Thus, the family was about 60 percent unemployed.

The Pratos live in a one-room house which they own. (A house is a necessary part of a dowry, and therefore most laborer families own them; one like Prato's can be rented for $4 a

6. This is the rate for a mature woman. Much housework is done by girls about 12 years old who live with the family and are on constant call. Such a girl is paid $4.84 in cash per month. In addition she may get an occasional "gift" of clothing.

month, however. About half the laborers have one-room and
the other half have two-room houses.) One-fourth of the floor
space is occupied by a huge "matrimonial" bed, the corn-husk
mattress of which is covered by an elaborately embroidered
spread and four enormous white pillows. Alongside of the bed
is a cot for Peppino. (Maria sleeps at her grandmother's two
doors away.) The other furniture consists of several straight-
back chairs, a table, and two coffin-like boxes, one for grain and
the other for "linens" (actually cottons). In winter tomatoes,
peppers, melons, and salami hang from the rafters. Other meat
from the family pig, especially sausages, is stored in crocks of
lard or brine. The house is unscreened and, although Montegrano is sprayed once or twice during the summer with DDT,
it is alive with flies.

The Pratos carry their water two or three hundred feet from
a neighborhood faucet which is part of a municipal sanitary
distribution system. They have nothing which can be called a
toilet, although there is a place a few steps from their doorway
to which they habitually retire. (They live on the periphery of
town; otherwise they would have to take more than a few steps
to find an alley where they could relieve themselves without
annoying others.)

They have no electricity. For light, they use an oil lamp.
Signora Prato makes bread by heating an oven with a brush-
wood fire, sweeping out the ashes, and putting the dough on
the hot stones. Other cooking she does in the open fireplace.

Prato has his first meal of the day at about nine o'clock, after
having worked two or three hours. It consists of a chunk of
bread and a handful of figs or tomatoes. At noon he has more of
the same. The night meal, eaten at eight or nine o'clock, is the
only one at which the family is likely to sit down together. It
consists of bread, a soup made of dry or green beans, a bit of
salami or sausage if any remains (the hog is slaughtered in December and the meat usually lasts until June or July), and fresh
or dry fruit.

Once a month on *festa* days—and not always then—the Pratos
have wine, cheese, fish, or meat. Their account book shows the

following expenditures for food, other than grain and flour, for
the entire year:

Macaroni and spaghetti (220 lbs.)	$16.85
Wine (7 gals.)	3.16
Potatoes	2.00
Meat (11 lbs.)	2.00
Olive Oil (2 qts.)	1.29
Sugar (7.5 lbs.)	.59
Fish (5 lbs.)	.45
Vinegar	.35
Onions	.16

A good deal of the Pratos' clothing is bought at the local fair
from Neapolitan dealers who import second-hand things from
the United States. Even by Montegrano standards the clothing
is inexpensive: a cotton house dress costs 35 to 50 cents, a shirt
slightly frayed at the collar 25 cents, a pair of child's jeans
mended at the knees 50 cents, and a man's woolen jacket $2.
Nevertheless, the Pratos do not have all the clothing they need.
Winter in Montegrano is wet and cold, but Prato's jacket is the
only warm outer garment the family possesses. Shoes are a
particular problem. A pair made by a local cobbler for rough
wear costs $5 and lasts less than two years.

Without a dowry, a Montegrano girl cannot make a satis-
factory marriage. For one in Maria Prato's position, a minimum
dowry consists of a *corredo* (trousseau) of "twelve," i.e., of
12 sheets and other household and personal supplies in proportion, the whole costing $375;[7] a piece of land worth $150, and
a one-room house. Although she has been engaged for a year,
Maria has been able to buy only five sheets and two blankets.
It will take her many years to accumulate her *corredo*, although
her family will do all it can to help. Even then, if her parents
are still alive, she will have no house. They would give her their
house and move into a rented one if they could pay rent.

Getting girls properly set up (*sistemate*) is a central preoccupation of all those who have them. When a peasant bride was

7. The minimum *corredo* is itemized in Appendix A, Table 8.

asked a week or two after her wedding what she would do with a windfall of income, she said that she would buy, among other things, a second house. "We have to think of the future," she explained, ". . . of the dowries for the girls."

Even among peasants the death rate is low (it was 9.3 per thousand for the commune as a whole in 1953). Peasant deaths, however, tend to occur at an earlier age than do others; a relatively large proportion of them are in infancy.[8]

There is much chronic illness: many live to old age without, apparently, ever feeling well. It can be taken for granted that in a family like the Pratos someone will always be ailing or partially disabled. Everyone suffers more or less from "liver trouble" (apparently a generic term referring to any abdominal discomfort); migraine headache, rheumatism, and toothache are common. As in most mountain districts to which sea breezes do not penetrate, there is a heavy incidence of goiter, especially among women. There is little tuberculosis or venereal disease.

About 350 families who are on the commune's poor list (the Pratos are not among these, much to their regret) get free medical care and such drugs as are necessary to save life.

Dr. Franco Gino, the health officer of the commune, says that at least 50 patients a year come to him suffering from nothing but hunger. These people present a difficult problem. Because their stomachs are shrunken they do not feel the pangs of hunger. If they were given a diet including milk, eggs, meat, together with vitamin injections, they would soon be restored to health. But then, their stomachs having returned to normal size, they would be able to feel hunger. And because there would be no possibility of their continuing the adequate diet, they would soon have to suffer the pain of returning to a state of semi-starvation. When such people come to him, Dr. Gino regretfully tells them that there is nothing he can do for them.

Having such small and uncertain incomes, laborers like Prato are constantly menaced by emergencies for which their ordinary economy cannot provide. The father may be unable to

8. Some details are given in Appendix A, Table 9.

work because of accident or illness, hail may destroy the grain crop, or the donkey or pig may die. If such calamities do not occur, there are sure to be minor crises. Prato, for example, never has enough savings or current income to pay his taxes or buy shoes.

Except in a few cases in which the head of the family is known to be a wine-bibber, laborers meet minor crises by running up small bills with merchants and artisans. There is no charge for this kind of credit and no difficulty about obtaining it for periods of a few weeks or months. Prato usually owes about $35 to various merchants.

The laborer may be able to get help from one of his employers in an emergency, but he cannot depend upon it. The feudal idea that a landowner ought to protect his workers has long since disappeared, but there are a few upper-class people who feeel some responsibility for one or two favored families. Last year when the Pratos were without bread, Don Paolo, one of the largest landowners, heard of their plight and sent them 200 pounds of wheat as a loan to be paid in labor the next spring. Prato was much affected by what he considered an extraordinary piece of kindness. Although he had always regarded Don Paolo as an unusual employer, he would not have thought of asking him for help.

Those who, like Prato, own a piece of land may meet emergencies by cutting oak trees or, in the most desperate circumstances, selling the land itself. Prato is reluctant to cut any of his few trees because he needs their branches for fuel and their leaves and acorns for livestock feed, and because he believes, rightly perhaps, that their removal would dry out the soil and so accelerate erosion.

There is a point, of course, beyond which the merchants will not carry a family. In such cases the commune offers no assistance (except, as noted, medical attention and drugs when necessary to save life) and neither does the church. The charity of relatives, friends, and neighbors is then the stricken family's only hope. These others are poor themselves, of course, and convention does not require them to accept responsibility for the welfare of others. Accordingly, those who must depend upon handouts fall to about as low a level of living as is possible. Nevertheless, no one starves, if by "starvation" is meant death resulting directly, rather than proximately, from lack of food. If there were a general crop failure, however, starvation would be widespread unless help came from the outside.

Many artisans are no better off than Prato. But the consumption pattern of the more prosperous artisans and merchants, and even of the office workers, professionals, and landowners, differs in amount rather than kind from that of the peasants. The well-off have larger houses with handsome varnished one-piece doors (the peasant's door is painted and made in four sections, so that a top section may be left open without letting animals in), but their houses are built and furnished in essentially the same way as those of the peasants and they are situated in every part of town. The well-off (as well as some of the peasants who are *not* well off) have recently installed two-burner stoves which use bottled gas. Most of their cooking, however, is done over open fireplaces. All of the well-off have electric lights, three-fourths have running water, and most have inside toilets. Very few have bathtubs, radios, refrigerators, or running hot water.

The peasants and artisans are aware that in northern Italy incomes are much higher. Few of them, however, have any hope of migrating. When he was asked why he had never gone north with his family, Prato said that he had never been fortunate enough to have a "call," i.e., an offer of work. Under a law passed in Fascist days, a villager who does not have a profession or independent means may not go to a city to look for work and he may not be offered work by an employer in the city except with the permission of the provincial authorities.[9]

9. The law also says that agricultural workers cannot, even in the town where they reside, "without a justified motive abandon the land to which destiny has assigned them." But unlike the prohibition on internal migration, this one is without practical effect. M. Gardner Clark, "Governmental Restrictions on Labor Mobility in Italy," *Industrial and Labor Relations Review,* Vol. 8, No. 1 (October 1954).

Since no northern employer knows of Prato's existence, he is not likely to get a "call" even if the authorities in Potenza are willing. If he goes looking for work in violation of the law, the *carabinieri* will find him sooner or later and send him home.

If they could do so, the people of Montegrano would migrate to the United States *en masse*. They know, however, that without a "call" from a relative, it is impossible even to get on the waiting list; for reasons that will appear, those who are already in the United States have lost interest in their Italian relatives. Migration to Argentina is somewhat easier, but the general opinion is that conditions there are not much better than in southern Italy. About Australia, another possibility, very little is known. Although the Italian government does not discourage migration abroad, as it does migration to the north, there is no place where the peasant can get a reasonably accurate account of the possibilities that exist.

⚡ ⚡ ⚡

Consumption patterns are changing very rapidly in Montegrano. These changes reflect others that are deep-lying and fundamental.

Twenty years ago every peasant woman wore a blouse and skirt. Nowadays only old women dress in this way. Peasant women who are not of the older generation wear print dresses that come secondhand from America. Formerly almost all women wore funereal black; deaths occurred frequently and the period of mourning was ten years. Now, because of antibiotics, deaths are few. Meanwhile, people have come to feel that one or two years is long enough to wear mourning.

Some peasant girls have permanent waves. A groom may give one to his bride as a wedding present. Twenty years ago peasants generally went barefoot. Now they all wear shoes. A man used to wear a jacket and pants and nothing else; now almost every man has some underwear and many even have stockings and a handkerchief. Formerly only a few prosperous peasants had holiday suits, and the pants and jackets of these seldom matched. Today most peasants have a suit for holiday wear, and a few are almost indistinguishable from the upper class as they stroll in the *piazza* on *festa* days.

Ten years ago peasants tanned their own leather and made their own shoes. Now they all buy their shoes at the store. Shirts used to be made at home. Now they are made by the tailors. Seamstresses and tailors work from pattern catalogues that show the styles in Rome, Paris, and New York.

A generation ago peasant women made little preparation for their babies. Now they see the midwife well in advance and have a supply of clean sheets and dressings ready for the parturition, and a *corredino* of diapers, undershirts, and the like for the new baby. Grandmothers are no longer listened to at childbirth; the midwife is in charge. Some peasant mothers even bathe their babies.

Even the most prosperous peasants bought nothing but salt and sardines at the store a few years ago. Montegrano's wheat is not hard enough to make good spaghetti, but even so spaghetti was made at home. Nowadays people buy *pasta* from the store or go without it. The peasant who has money to spend at the store buys the same foods, including canned ones, that are bought by the upper class.

Several years ago there was no bar and no movie in Montegrano. Now there are two bars and two movies. Some peasants feel deprived if they do not see a movie twice a month. A few go occasionally to a bar for a cup of *espresso* coffee.

These changes are not the product of greater prosperity. Most peasants are probably poorer than they were a generation ago: they have less to eat and less in savings. Soil erosion has left Montegrano's land base smaller than it was then, and the gradual depletion of the fertility of the soil that remains has led to a less intensive agriculture. The population to be supported by the reduced resources, however, is slightly larger than it was a generation ago.

One cause of these changes has been improvement of highways by public works projects. Isolated as it still is, Montegrano is more accessible to the cities than formerly. Salesmen who would not have thought of journeying there a few years back stop more or less regularly now.

Another cause of change (and also an effect of it) is reduction of cultural distance between the peasant and the outside world. A generation ago peasants seem to have taken it for granted that they were a different breed than other folk. Some of them— Prato, for example—still do. But many see no difference between themselves and others except that the others are better off. Those who take this view are unwilling to wear a peasant costume or to be set apart in other ways.

Paolo Vitello, a laborer who works at a forge, may be taken as an example of the new-style consumer. He spent some time in the cities of the north during his military service and has not forgotten what he saw there.[10] Although his income is twenty percent less than Prato's, he somehow manages to spend a great deal more.[11] His house has electric lights, bottled gas, and a toilet—all luxuries which Prato thinks are forever beyond him. He buys a bit of meat, fish, cheese, and sugar now and then— something Prato almost never does—and when he feels flush he buys his wife a handkerchief, his youngest child a toy or a cookie, or himself a beer, a cigarette, or a sixteen-cent lottery

10. Prato was not in military service and he has only once seen a big city. No doubt Vitello's military experience accounts in part for his more sophisticated standards of consumption. But it would be a mistake to suppose that war-time travel accounts in general for the changes that are underway in Montegrano. Some villagers saw more of the world than did Vitello and were utterly unaffected by what they saw. Moreover, some very important changes were underway before the war: peasants had begun to practice birth control, for example, at least a decade before the war. Perhaps the decisive difference between Vitello and Prato is not in travel experience but in the fact that Vitello (although the objective circumstances of his early life, including schooling, were not much different from Prato's) has always thought of himself as an artisan and a townsman rather than as a peasant. There are, however, new-style consumers who cannot make the slightest claim to being anything but peasants.

11. The Vitello family's expenses for the year are summarized in Appendix A, Table 10. During the year for which accounts were kept Vitello went deeply into debt. It was obvious that the next year he would have to earn more or spend less.

ticket. Prato, it is safe to say, has never in his life bought a luxury. On holidays Vitello takes his ease in the public square, dressed in a black suit like a gentleman. Prato has no holiday suit. Vitello's wife suffers from chronic headaches; she goes frequently to the doctor and buys vitamins and other drugs. Prato's wife is also chronically ill, but her medical expenses for the year consisted of the price of two aspirin tablets. Vitello hopes to persuade a relative in Naples who is a tailor there to take one of his boys as an apprentice. Although Prato is deeply dissatisfied, the possibility that his children might leave Montegrano and become something other than peasants seems so remote to him as not to be worth consideration.

Now that buying things from the store has become one of the possible ways of showing love for one's family, not to do so seems to a new-style consumer like coldness or indifference. One evening, Pasquale Dura, an intermittently employed farm laborer with seven children, came home with a radio for which he had promised to pay eight dollars a month. At first his wife was furious and demanded that he take it back at once. Then he explained that, although he could go to the public square for amusement, she and the children had to be always at home; it would be good, he said, for them to have one thing that would give them pleasure—one thing to relieve *la misèria*. In fact, he went on, it was not fair to the children that they should grow up with nothing at all. Who knows? Perhaps they might learn something from the radio. When she heard the explanation, his wife was touched. The Duras kept the radio and it at once became the active agent of further change. "I was in mourning," Signora Dura explained later, "but when we decided to keep the radio, of course I took the mourning off. After all, you don't have a radio going in the house and wear mourning at the same time."

✦   ✦   ✦

When the peasant speaks of *la misèria*, he refers first to his hard physical labor, to his patched rags, and to the bread that is often all he has to eat. Cruel as it is, however, his poverty does not entirely account for his chronic melancholy. Many peasants are idle a good part of the time because there is no work for them to do. Those who have a little land trudge up and down the mountainside driving a pig to pasture or gathering firewood, but this is not exhausting labor. Much of the peasant's incessant going and coming is nothing but a way of passing time. "Our house is so small and crowded that we couldn't stand each other if we were cooped up in it all the time," an old woman explained when asked why she and her crippled husband struggled through the summer heat to a barren garden patch at the foot of the mountain. Winter temperatures are seldom below freezing, and although many people are extremely uncomfortable for lack of clothing, no one freezes or suffers serious injury. Many are ill from dietary deficiencies, but no one starves to death and few are painfully hungry more than now and then.

In part the peasant's melancholy is caused by worry. Having no savings, he must always dread what is likely to happen. What for others are misfortunes are for him calamities. When their hog strangled on its tether, a laborer and his wife were desolate. The woman tore her hair and beat her head against a wall while the husband sat mute and stricken in a corner. The loss of the hog meant they would have no meat that winter, no grease to spread on bread, nothing to sell for cash to pay taxes, and no possibility of acquiring a pig the next spring. Such blows may fall at any time. Fields may be washed away in a flood. Hail may beat down the wheat. Illness may strike. To be a peasant is to stand helpless before these possibilities.

But neither his present hunger nor his anticipation of worse to come fully accounts for the peasant's deep dissatisfaction. There are primitive societies in which the level of biological well-being is even lower, but in which people are not chronically unhappy. What makes the difference between a low level of living and *la miseria* comes from culture. Unlike the primitive, the peasant feels himself part of a larger society which he is "in" but not altogether "of." He lives in a culture in which it is very important to be admired, and he sees that by its standards he cannot be admired in the least; by these standards he and everything about him are contemptible or ridiculous. Knowing this, he is filled with loathing for his lot and with anger for the fates which assigned him to it.

"Getting ahead" and "making a good figure" are two of the central themes of the peasant's existence. But he sees that no matter how hard he works he can never get ahead. Other people can use their labor to advantage, but not he. If he has a a bit of land, he may conceal the waste of his time from others and perhaps even from himself by some monumental labor—terracing a hillside with soil carried on his back from the valley, for example. He knows, however, that in the end he will be no better off than before.

The knowledge that no matter how hard he struggles he will remain behind (*indietro*) is galling. Prato, for example, can never save enough to get his daughter properly married. In his eyes it is the impossibility of improving his position which distinguishes the peasant from others. "The peasant," he said, "always keeps his place; others have the possibility of improving themselves." In only two of 320 stories told by 16 Montegrano peasants who were given Thematic Apperception Tests [12] did a family prosper by thrift or enterprise, and even in these cases the success was not great enough to raise it out

12. The Thematic Apperception Test is a method widely used by the psychologist to reveal the dominant emotions, sentiments, and conflicts of a personality. The subject is shown a series of 20 pictures and asked to make up stories about them on the spur of the moment. The pictures are of varying degrees of ambiguity (one is actually a blank card). The subject interprets them in ways which consciously and unconsciously shed light on his sentiments, values, wants, and preoccupations. Psychologists can infer from clues in the stories some important aspects of the storyteller's personality. Here, however, the TAT has been used mainly for what it may tell abouc ethos rather than personality. The pictures used were prepared by Dr. Henry A. Murray of the Harvard Psychological Clinic.

of the peasant class. In the TAT stories, dramatic success came only as a gift of fortune: a rich gentleman gave a poor boy a violin, a rich gentlewoman adopted an abandoned child, and so on.

By the standards of the larger society, the peasant's work, food, and clothing all symbolize his degradation. It is on this account, as much as for biological reasons, that he finds them unsatisfying and even hateful. Southern Italians attach great importance to being mannerly (*civile*); the peasant feels that he is the very opposite: association with earth and animals, he thinks, has made him dirty and animal-like. "We poor peasants," one said, "work from morning until night always touching the earth and always covered with mud." Prato's jacket keeps him reasonably warm, but it marks him as one to whom no respect is due. When he was asked his impressions of a big city, he spoke of the way people dressed. "In the city," he said, "everyone dresses the same and you cannot tell whether a man is a peasant or not."

Peasants often complain that they have no recreation, and they speak as if this were as much of a hardship as hard work or hunger. Taken at its face value, this complaint is ridiculous. Except at the busy times of planting and harvesting, there is nothing to prevent the peasants from playing as much as they like. What is to stop them from dancing and singing? Or from playing cards? Or telling stories? What the peasant lacks is not opportunity for recreation, but opportunity for those particular kinds of recreation—having coffee in the bar in the public square, for example—which are *civile* and which would therefore identify them as persons entitled to respect and admiration.

La misèria, it seems safe to conclude, arises as much or more from social as from biological deprivations. This being the case, there is no reason to expect that a moderate increase in income (if by some miracle that could be brought about) would make the atmosphere of the village less heavy with melancholy. On the contrary, unless there were accompanying changes in social structure and culture, increasing incomes would probably bring with them increasing discontent.[13]

13. An instructive contrast may be drawn between Montegrano and the Spanish village vividly described by J. A. Pitt-Rivers in *The People of the Sierra*, Weidenfeld and Nicolson, London, 1954. The Andalusian village seems to be about as poor as Montegrano, but its mood is not melancholy. This difference is perhaps both cause and effect of other differences: the Andalusian peasant identifies strongly with his village, his kinship and friendship ties are numerous and significant, and he does not feel humiliated by his social status. Boasting and vanity are striking features of Andalusian (but not of Montegrano) culture; perhaps these are compensatory devices by which the Spaniard protects his ego from total destruction.

4

Class Relations

ALTHOUGH the political incapacity of Montegrano cannot be accounted for by class conflict, the peasant's status and the relations among the classes are undoubtedly important features of the situation.

The seven occupations listed in the previous chapter may be grouped into three social classes:

1. *Peasants.*[1] This class consists of those who do manual labor on the land, viz., farm laborers and farmers, and includes somewhat more than two-thirds of the population. Manual labor is degrading in the southern Italian ethos, and labor on the land, together with personal service, is especially so. There is therefore a crucial status difference between peasants (and servants, who are recruited from among them) and others. Only the gypsies, who belong to a different caste, have lower status than the peasants.

2. *Artisans and merchants.* The members of this class do manual labor, but not on the land and not as servants. About 10 percent of the population belong to this class.

3. *Upper classes.* The defining characteristic of an upper

1. The word *contadino*, translated here as "peasant," is used in Montegrano in two senses: (a) to denote a status class, viz., all those who do manual labor on the land, and (b) to denote a tenure class, viz., those who own land (and work it themselves), as distinguished from farm laborers.

class person (*persona per bene* or *benestante*) is that he does no manual labor. Two other characteristics are usually factually associated with this defining one: (a) the upper class person has a somewhat higher level of living; there are, however, some farmers and merchants whose incomes are much higher than those of some upper-class people; and (b) he has had at least five, and usually eight or more, grades of schooling. The office workers, professionals, and landed proprietors—together about 10 percent of the population—comprise the upper class.

Within the upper class a sharp distinction is made between those who are gentlemen (*galantuomini*) and those who are not. Being a gentleman is altogether a matter of birth; regardless of occupation, education, or income, one is a gentleman if one's father was one.[2] The situation of the gentry is no different from that of other upper class people, except that they receive greater deference: they are always addressed by the title "Don" or "Donna" coupled with their Christian names—"Don Paolo" or "Donna Maria." Priests have the title *ex officio*.

The gentry are sometimes referred to as "noble families," but strictly speaking, only the Baron di Longo has a title. His uncle is said to have bought it in Fascist times.

In some southern towns, apparently, there is much jealousy, backbiting, and feuding among the gentry. This is not the case in Montegrano and has not been for at least a generation. There are certain long-standing family rivalries, but on the whole the gentlemen get along with each other fairly well.

In some towns also, apparently, the artisans and peasants are mutually hostile: in such places a political candidate who is favored by one class will be opposed by the other automatically. In Montegrano, however, there is not this sense of opposed identities either in politics or in other spheres. Peasants

2. In one instance in Montegrano, the category "*galantuomo*" cuts across class lines: Don Alfredo, a merchant who sells fine cloth, is a gentleman. His business is peculiar, however, in that his customers are almost all of the upper class. It is hardly conceivable that he would be called "Don" if he sold cheese and sardines to peasants.

and artisans mix freely on friendly terms. Peasant dances are attended by artisans and artisan dances by peasants.

No fundamental status distinction is made between peasants who own land and those who do not. As the previous chapter explained, few peasants have more than a small plot, and the manner of life of these is hardly different from that of the landless. Even the few relatively well-off peasants do not constitute a separate social circle, and when one of them goes to a laborer's wedding feast he is not—as an upper class person always is—put at the head of the table with the bride and groom. No particular attention is paid to him.

Importance *is* attached to the difference between town and country manners. The country-dwelling peasant, although he is generally much better off than the town-dwelling peasant (in fact, he lives in the country *because* he has enough land and livestock to require his presence there), is often regarded as a "rube" (*cafone*). His speech, dress, and country ways are ridiculed by those who themselves have no land or livestock and sometimes not even a mouthful of bread. When a procession forms to escort an engaged couple from the bride's home to the church, a town girl does not walk beside a country boy. A town boy may walk beside a country girl, however.

↗ ↗ ↗

A Montegrano family is always in danger of falling in the social scale from one generation to the next. This is especially true in the upper class, of course. If the father dies young, the children may drop into the merchant-artisan class despite the widow's heroic efforts to keep them from manual labor. If an eldest son is wayward—if he drinks or does not study, for example—he may be the ruin of the whole line. For the family invests all of its resources in him, expecting that when he becomes a doctor, lawyer, or civil servant (these are almost the only possibilities a southerner recognizes) he will help his younger brothers and sisters. If he fails to get a degree, the patrimony has been wasted and there is no opportunity for the younger ones. If there are two sons and a daughter, the young-est son and his wife and children are likely to move down in the social scale. The elder son gets the education. The daughter gets half the family's land as a dowry; this (with what her husband has) sets her branch of the family up well. The younger son, then, gets less education than his brother and less capital than his sister; his children, accordingly, will not be as well off as theirs.

Those upper class people who can do so leave Montegrano to live in a city. The village affords a living for only one lawyer, one doctor, one pharmacist, and several civil servants. There are more professionals than this in the village at any one time, but the others are only waiting for a place to open up some-where else. An upper class man remains in Montegrano only if he has some special advantage there which it would be unthink-able to relinquish—if he is *the* doctor or *the* lawyer—or if it is simply not possible for him to make a living in the city. Thus a younger son who did not go beyond the fifth grade may remain in Montegrano as the "proprietor" of several acres of land which are, of course, worked by tenants. Feeling keenly his inferiority to an older brother who has become, perhaps, a customs official in Genoa, the stay-at-home takes little part in family or public affairs. Decisions are left to the educated brother who comes once a year from Genoa.

The 26 gentry families of Montegrano include 59 active men (that is, men between the ages of 20 and 65 who are not in-capacitated by illness). Only 19 of these live in the village.

In the lower classes there is the same pervasive fear that in the next generation the family may fall into a lower class. The artisan fears that his children may have to work on the land. The petty peasant proprietor knows that if he has a large fam-ily (especially a large family of girls!) his children will drop into the ranks of the landless or near-landless. Even Prato, a laborer, worries that his daughter, for lack of a *corredo*, may have to marry someone who has neither house nor land and is therefore "no better than a gypsy." Only the poorest of the poor—the laborer with nothing but a mattock—is immune from these fears; his is the only status which cannot be worsened in the next generation.

In every class there is some possibility, however slight, of upward mobility. The son of a landless laborer occasionally marries well and uses his wife's dowry to become a petty cultivator or the owner of a piece of equipment that he can rent out with his labor. The peasant proprietor seizes an opportunity to send his son into trade (for a sentimental attachment to the land to stand in the way of such a move is inconceivable). The daughter of an artisan may marry a teacher and the artisan's son may have the good fortune to become a merchant or a government clerk.

For the landless peasant to learn a trade and become an artisan is possible under unusual circumstances. The boy may find an artisan who will take him as an apprentice, for an apprentice is paid nothing or next to nothing. In the usual case, however, his family will not support him during the four or five years it takes to learn a trade; on the contrary, it expects him to contribute to its support, especially if he has sisters who need dowries. Even if he somehow manages to complete an apprenticeship, the peasant may have to work in the fields, for there are many more blacksmiths, shoemakers, tailors, and the like than the village can support. A boy who learns his trade in Montegrano is not usually skillful enough to earn a living by it in the city, where standards are much more exacting.

A boy who finishes eight grades of school may become a policeman. (Officially only five are required, but the competition is so keen that eight are virtually necessary.) For a peasant this represents a great advance: a member of the *carabinieri* is well-clothed and well-fed and paid 85 cents a day in cash—enough to enable him to support his old mother or provide his sister with a dowry. The *carabiniere* may not marry until he reaches 30 and he is likely to be stationed in a backward village like Montegrano (he is never stationed in his native place) where his children can get little schooling. At 45 he retires with a pension so small that, unless he has acquired some land by inheritance or marriage, there is nothing he can do but live in a remote village where living costs are low. To an overwhelming extent, the police of Italy are drawn from the villages of the south.

Occasionally a boy moves from near the bottom of the social scale to near the top. This may be done in only one way: formal education. If he completes 12 grades of school—which is to say, if his family can afford to send him out of town to school for seven grades beyond the fifth grade—a peasant boy may become a village teacher at the age of 18. Then, if he is lucky, he may marry a not-very-marriageable upper class girl who will bring him a good dowry. For the few relatively prosperous peasant families this is a well-established way of providing for a second son: the expense of the boy's schooling may be a hardship for the family, but the return on it begins fairly soon. Most teachers in villages like Montegrano come from the lower classes.

So do the priests. A boy must go eight years beyond elementary school before the Church might finance his further education. Thus, only those who can afford to become teachers can afford to become priests; lower class boys who might be tempted to enter a seminary merely to get an education are in this way excluded. Priests are drawn from the strata of those well enough off to go to *media* school but not well enough off to become doctors or lawyers. The identification of the priesthood with this strata is complete; upper class boys do not think of becoming priests.

In rare cases a peasant may become a professional. For example, a poor peasant died of war injuries leaving a small pension and a plot of land. Although illiterate herself, his widow determined to educate her two sons. The elder became a teacher. He helped the younger through school, and the mother sold her farm bit by bit to keep him in medical school in Bologna. Now the brothers, one of whom is the Communist mayor of Basso, are called "Don" by the lower class, and in some important respects, at least, are treated as equals by the other professionals.[3]

3. In 1950–55, 62 Montegrano boys and girls went beyond the fitfh grade, i.e., went out of the village to continue their schooling for at

The peasant can never entirely transcend his social origins, however. An engineer, the son of an impoverished petty proprietor, confessed that he would resent it very much if a lower class person were to ask his fiancee to dance. "I am a socialist and I know better," he said, "but I can't help feeling above the peasants. I would resent it even if the person who asked her to dance were the son of a peasant . . . even if he were better educated than I. To us he is still a peasant."

The rate of economic progress in southern Italy is such that merely to retain its place in the income and status hierarchy a family must invest more and more in its children. Many lower class people sense that unless their children get a much better start in life than did children five or ten years ago, they will surely fall behind. To live in Montegrano, some of them see, is a more serious disadvantage now than formerly. It used to be, for example, that one could become a *carabiniere* after only five grades of school. Now that it usually takes eight years—three more than the local school offers—this avenue is closed to all but a few.

Seeing these changes, most lower class couples are making an effort to limit the size of their families. The ideal family, they say, consists of two children: one is "not really a family"; more cannot be given a decent start. This is a strategy which the upper classes, faced with the same problem, adopted a generation or two ago.

*   *   *

When a gentleman of Montegrano buys a melon or a basket of tomatoes in the public square, he hands it wordlessly to the

least one year. Seven were the sons or daughters of professionals or landed proprietors, 19 of office workers, nine of merchants, 14 of artisans, five of peasant owners, and eight of farm laborers. Of the last two categories, peasant cultivators and laborers, four went into religious training, which costs very little; four had fathers killed in the war and mothers pensioned; three were helped by siblings who were policemen or prison guards in towns where there were schools; and one was supported by his mother who worked as a housemaid in Naples. Of the 62, 16 were girls. The girls were all upper-class.

nearest peasant boy, woman, or man, who carries it to his home as a matter of course. He hands his burden to any peasant with whom he is acquainted, and there is no thought on either side of payment for the specific service. The peasant wants to be polite and amiable (*civile*) and he knows that a time will come when the gentleman can give or withhold a favor or an injury. (Even those peasants who are not anti-clerical will not lift a finger to assist a nun carrying a heavy burden to the orphanage at the top of the mountain. The nuns are upper class women, but they have no capacity to do the peasant a favor or an injury. Priests, of course, *can* do favors and injuries, and their bundles are carried for them.)

Twenty years ago a gentleman did not hesitate to ask a peasant to chop his winter's wood supply without payment. Even today a gentleman who needs a donkey expects a peasant "friend" to supply one without charge; ordinarily the peasant himself goes with the donkey or sends one of his family, for if the handling of the donkey is left to the gentleman's servant and the animal is injured, there will be no recompense.

When the tax collector wants his grapes harvested, he tells two or three peasants to harvest them. For their day's work, he gives them two or three pounds of grapes each. They do not think that their taxes would be higher if they refused, but they have a feeling that somehow it is best to stay on the collector's good side.

At Christmas a peasant who lives in the country brings a rooster or a basket of eggs to each of the two or three gentlemen who are his particular "friends." One of the gentlemen may be his godfather (in this case he brings him a rooster on his name-day as well); another may once have written a letter for him or, perhaps, for his father; the third may be an occasional employer. The gentleman gives the peasant nothing; he accepts the gift because it is the pleasant custom of the peasants to give gentlemen gifts.

The peasant's gifts are not without material value. But the giving and taking are significant in a symbolic way as well. The peasant would be embarrassed to go to the gentleman's house to pay a purely social call. If the peasant woman carries a few eggs to the gentlewoman, she provides an occasion for the call and thus makes possible a friendly interchange between the two. The eggs, by making clear that the relationship is not between equals, permit the relationship to exist.

Although the peasant is less likely than the gentleman to minimize the material value of the gift, he too sees the giving and taking as a symbolic act. But nowadays he does not always take kindly to having his inferiority ritually established at his expense. A peasant woman remarked sourly,

Each one of them [the gentry] thinks he's a pope or a cardinal and it is seldom they do a favor for the poor. One must go to them always with something in one's hands and knock on the door with one's feet.

There are some peasants in Montegrano who think the gentry are by nature superior and therefore have the right to demand service and deference. Prato, for example, says:

Yes, certainly the well-off are better. They are richer and so of course they are better and the rest of us have to be under them.

When she was asked how it happens that in Montegrano some people are rich while others are poor, Laura, a laborer's wife, said:

Who knows about things which have to do with the creation of the world? [4]

Most peasants, however, give a very different answer to such questions. The rich, they say, are those whose grandfathers, at a time of great distress a century ago, bought land from others who were foolish enough, or hard-pressed enough, to sell "for a handful of figs." In other cases, the rich got their money by cheating, stealing, or exploiting the poor.

"It is not brains," Anna said. "I have as much brains as any of them. The only difference is that I have never a cent that I

4. The Baron di Longo takes the same view. "An oak tree will always produce acorns and an olive tree olives," he is quoted as having said at a political rally.

could put to work for me. If I had a little, I believe I could put it to work for me too."

When the Baron di Longo reproved one his tenants for sending his boy to school, the tenant said to him, "But Baron, you send your son to school."

"Of course," the Baron replied. "But who is going to work my land if all the peasants go off to school?"

"Why, your son could work it," the peasant said.

ʃ   ʃ   ʃ

Class relations in Montegrano are nevertheless amicable by Italian standards. One reason for this is that in the last two or three generations the upper-class has not monopolized the land. The Baron owns numerous farms but they are all worked by tenants. None of the other "landed proprietors" has more than a few acres of cultivated land—no more, in fact, than is owned by the more prosperous peasants. Moreover, the standard of living of the upper class differs in amount rather than in kind from that of the lower class. The peasant can easily see that the gentleman, for all his advantages, lives in much the same world as he.

Tradition is another reason. In some towns the upper class has always been brutal toward the peasants. This has not been the case in Montegrano. The leading families have been by tradition, if not actually considerate, at least not cruel.

Nearby Basso presents an interesting contrast. It lies in the valley where the land is rich and irrigable. Most of the land is in large holdings and worked by day laborers. For as long as anyone can remember the landowners of Basso have acted as if the peasant did not exist. Gentlemen who walk down the street in Basso see only gentlemen. There has been organization of labor from time to time in Basso and bitter strikes. In Montegrano, there could not well be organization since there are no big employers, but apart from this, in Montegrano the atmosphere is different. In Montegrano, a gentleman speaks to a peasant when he meets him on the road, and he may even play cards with him in the bar of an afternoon.

All the same, some Montegrano peasants hate the upper class fiercely.

The upper class are always squashing the peasant under their feet. They treat us like animals. They only care about eating well and sleeping. They don't care about us. They never even get near us. The only way you can get near them is when you bring them something; then they are all smiles and full of welcome. I say that we are all the same—all sons of God. But they spit in our faces.

Few speak so violently. But all resent in some degree the airs of superiority which the *signore* who sits in the breeze shows to the laborer on whose work his bread depends.

The gentleman, many peasants say, is apt to be grasping and haughty.

If you bring a little thing to them and ask a favor, they'll often give you what you ask, but for that they'll have to insult you first. For example, they'll say, 'Why didn't your mother send you to school?' As if they didn't know.

The peasant is apt to be embarrassed in the presence of upper class people by his lack of graceful manners and his uneducated speech. This may make him extremely sensitive to real or fancied insults. As Don Franco, the doctor, has observed in a sketch he wrote of village life:

The poor are very touchy and they have a right to be. One can banter only in town among the well-off. Even if you watch yourself when you speak to a peasant and take care to make no allusions to his poverty, a poor man will spot an allusion which escapes you (for it not to escape you, you would have to be poor yourself!) and then you realize how it affects him and you too feel bad and become melancholy when he, out of respect to you who are a gentleman, does not answer back rudely and even understands that you did not do it on purpose.

Some gentlemen are unaware of the peasant's plight or indifferent to it. Others, like Don Franco, are acutely aware of it and very much distressed by it. But the gentleman who is sensitive to the peasant's feeling may be—perhaps for this very reason—little able to communicate with him. Such a one may feel a weight of guilt toward the peasant, as if he were responsible for his misery. He wants the peasant's good opinion—his forgiveness, and he is often vehement in denouncing those—the capitalists, perhaps—who are supposed to be in league against the peasant. But the gentleman does not and cannot talk with the peasant as one reasonable human being to another. Perhaps this is because he does not really believe that the peasant is a reasonable human being like himself: he pities the peasant for being less than human and blames his own class, the system, and destiny for having made the peasant so, but accepts the fact. In part also, perhaps, this is because the gentleman must protect his feelings against the assaults which the peasant knowingly or unknowingly makes upon them; pretending that he does not understand the peasant and deliberately causing the peasant to misunderstand him are ways of doing this.

A laborer's wife who was bitten in the hand by a donkey went to Don Franco. While he was treating her she asked if she were eligible for unemployment compensation. According to her, he laughed.

"That's a fine one," he said. "You go and get your hand bitten, and now you think I should sign for you to get help from the Welfare Office."

The doctor knew that the town's welfare fund was insufficient to meet the most pressing demands upon it. He assumed —probably rightly—that he could not explain to a peasant woman that others had greater need than she. He adopted a bantering tone because (one may assume) doing so would avoid the necessity of serious explanation or discussion.

The woman, however, was angered both by the doctor's jocular-ironic tone and his suggestion that she had injured herself purposely. Did he think she enjoyed being bitten and not being able to work? she asked.

After he had bandaged her, Don Franco gave the woman a prescription for penicillin. Later she returned in accordance with his instructions to have the bandage changed. By then, she had a fever. As long as the fever continued she should take penicillin, the doctor told her. The pharmacist had refused to give her credit and the prescription had never been filled, but she did not tell the doctor this. Why? a visitor asked.

"Oh," she said, "those two [the doctor and the pharmacist] are in cahoots."

Thus, even in a town where class relations are amicable by tradition and even in the case of the one who, of all gentlemen, ought to be on understanding terms with the peasants (for Don Franco is at once a physician, the leading representative of a party dedicated to ending class differences, and a man gifted with the insight and sensitivity of a literary artist), a thick wall of misunderstanding and suspicion separates the upper from the lower class.

Although many take trouble to conceal it, there is, one suspects, a deep well of hostility toward the upper class within every peasant. This at least is the belief of the upper class itself. In another of his sketches of village life, Don Franco speaks of the sadness that comes over a certain upper class person when he hears the church bells toll in the evening. For the peasant however, Don Franco observes, the sound of the bells brings a corresponding satisfaction: it reminds him that gentlemen too must die.

5

A Predictive Hypothesis

A VERY simple hypothesis will make intelligible all of the behavior about which questions have been raised and will enable
an observer to predict how the Montegranesi will act in concrete circumstances. The hypothesis is that the Montegranesi
act as if they were following this rule:

> Maximize the material, short-run advantage of the nuclear family;
> assume that all others will do likewise.

One whose behavior is consistent with this rule will be
called an "amoral familist." The term is awkward and somewhat
imprecise (one who follows the rule is without morality only in
relation to persons outside the family—in relation to family
members, he applies standards of right and wrong; one who has
no family is of course an "amoral individualist"), but no other
term seems better.

In this chapter, some logical implications of the rule are set
forth. It will be seen that these describe the facts of behavior in
the Montegrano district. The coincidence of facts and theory
does not "prove" the theory. However, it does show that the
theory will explain (in the sense of making intelligible and
predictable) much behavior without being contradicted by
any of the facts at hand.

1. *In a society of amoral familists, no one will further the
interest of the group or community except as it is to his private*

advantage to do so. In other words, the hope of material gain in the short-run will be the only motive for concern with public affairs.

This principle is of course consistent with the entire absence of civic improvement associations, organized charities, and leading citizens who take initiative in public service.[1]

A teacher who is a member of a leading family explained,

I have always kept myself aloof from public questions, especially political ones. I think that all the parties are identical and those who belong to them—whether Communist, Christian Democrat, or other—are men who seek their own welfare and well-being. And then too, if you want to belong to one party, you are certain to be on the outs with the people of the other party.

Giovanni Gola, a merchant of upper-class origins, has never been a member of a political party because "It isn't convenient for me—I might lose some business."

Gola does not think of running for office because:

I have all I can do to look after my own affairs. I do enough struggling in my business not to want to add to it in any political struggling. Once in office there would be a constant demand for favors or attentions. I'd have to spend all my time looking after other people's affairs . . . my own would have to be neglected. I don't feel like working hard any more. I am no longer young. [He is in his late forties.]

Those who run for office, Gola says, do so for private advantage.

1. The importance of voluntary associations in the United States has been explained by their function in facilitating social mobility. This explanation is not incompatible with the one given above.

Those who belong to "do-good" organizations secure gratifications (e.g., status, power, neighborly associations, etc.) which have nothing to do with the public-spirited purposes for which the organizations exist. Even so, these public-spirited purposes are not unimportant in the motivations of the participants. Moreover, most of the self-regarded ends which are served do not relate to material gain, or at least not to material gain in the short-run.

They get the office, and then they look after themselves. Some take office so as to be able to say, "I am the mayor." But really there isn't much honor attaching to an office; people here don't even respect the President of the Republic. In F—, the mayor wants to be mayor so that he can keep the population down.

2. *In a society of amoral familists only officials will concern themselves with public affairs, for only they are paid to do so. For a private citizen to take a serious interest in a public problem will be regarded as abnormal and even improper.*

Cavalier Rossi, one of the largest landowners of Montegrano, and the mayor of the nearby town of Capa, sees the need for many local public improvements. If he went to the prefect in Potenza as mayor of Capa, they would listen to him, he says. But if he went as a private citizen of Montegrano, they would say, "Who are you?" As a private citizen he might help a worker get a pension, but as for schools, hospitals, and such things, those are for the authorities to dole out. A private citizen can do nothing.

The trouble is only partly that officials will not listen to private citizens. To a considerable extent it is also that private citizens will not take responsibility in public matters. As Rossi explains,

There are no leaders in Montegrano. People's minds are too unstable; they aren't firm; they get excited and make a decision. Then the next day they have changed their minds and fallen away. It's more or less the same way in Capa. There is lots of talk, but no real personal interest. It always come to this: the mayor has to do it. They expect the mayor to do everything and to get everything—to make a world.

Farmuso, the director of the school district and formerly the Communist mayor of a town in another province, is earnest, energetic, and intelligent. He listed several things which might be done to improve the situation in Montegrano, but when he was asked if he could bring influence to bear to get any of them done, he said that he could not. "I am interested only in the schools," he explained. "If I wanted to exert influence, with whom would I talk? In Vernande there are six teachers in two rooms, but no money for improvements. I have talked to the mayor and others, but I can't get anything even there."

The feeling that unofficial action is an intrusion upon the sphere of the state accounts in some measure both for Mayor Spomo's haughty officiousness and for the failure of private persons to interest themselves in making stop-gap arrangements for a school and a hospital. In nearby Basso a reclamation project will increase vegetable production and make possible the establishment of a canning factory. The large landowners of Basso will not join together to build a factory, however, even though it might be a good investment. It is the right and the duty of the state to build it.

3. *In a society of amoral familists there will be few checks on officials, for checking on officials will be the business of other officials only.*

When Farmuso, the school director, was asked what he would do if it came to his attention that a public official took bribes, he said that if the bribery were in his own department he would expose it at once. However, if it occurred outside his department, he would say nothing, for in that case it would be none of his concern.

A young schoolteacher, answering the same question, said that even if he could prove the bribery he would do nothing. "You are likely to be made a martyr," he explained. "It takes courage to do it. There are so many more dishonest people than honest ones that they can gang up on you . . . twist the facts so that you appear to be the guilty one. Remember Christ and the Pharisees."

A leading merchant would not expose bribery, because "Sooner or later someone would come to me and tell me it would be good if I didn't."

4. *In a society of amoral familists, organization (i.e., deliberately concerted action) will be very difficult to achieve and maintain. The inducements which lead people to contribute their activity to organizations are to an important degree unselfish (e.g., identification with the purpose of the organiza-*

tion) and they are often non-material (e.g., the intrinsic interest of the activity as a "game"). Moreover, it is a condition of successful organization that members have some trust in each other and some loyalty to the organization. In an organization with high morale it is taken for granted that they will make small sacrifices, and perhaps even large ones, for the sake of the organization.

The only formal organizations which exist in Montegrano—the church and the state—are of course provided from the outside; if they were not, they could not exist. Inability to create and maintain organization is clearly of the greatest importance in retarding economic development in the region.[2]

Despite the moral and other resources it can draw upon from the outside, the church in Montegrano suffers from the general inability to maintain organization. There are two parishes, each with its priest. Rivalry between the priests is so keen that neither can do anything out of the ordinary without having obstacles placed in his way by the other, and cooperation between them is wholly out of the question. (On one occasion they nearly came to blows in the public square; on another the saint of one parish was refused admittance to the church of the other when the *festa*-day procession stopped there on its route.) When some young men tried to organize a chapter of Catholic Action, a lay association to carry Catholic principles into secular life, they encountered so much sabotage from the feuding priests, neither of whom was willing to tolerate an activity for which the other might receive some credit, that the project was soon abandoned.

2. Max Weber remarked in *The Protestant Ethic and the Rise of Capitalism* (Allen and Unwin edition, London, 1930, p. 57) that "the universal reign of absolute unscrupulousness in the pursuit of selfish interests by the making of money has been a specific characteristic of precisely those countries whose bourgeois-capitalistic development, measured according to Occidental standards, has remained backward. As every employer knows, the lack of *coscienziosita* of the laborers of such countries, for instance Italy as compared with Germany, has been, and to a certain extent still is, one of the principal obstacles to their capitalistic development."

The Montegranesi might be expected not to make good soldiers. However brave he may be, the amoral familist does not
win battles. Soldiers fight from loyalty to an organization, especially the primary groups of "buddies," not from self-interest
narrowly conceived.

Lack of attachment even to kindred has impeded emigration
and indirectly economic development. In the half century
prior to 1922, there was heavy emigration from Montegrano to
the United States and later to Argentina. In general, however,
ties between the emigrants and those who remained at home
were not strong enough to support "chains" of emigration.
Hundreds of Montegranesi live in the hope that a brother or
uncle in America will send a "call," but such calls rarely come.
People are perplexed when their relatives in America do not
answer their letters. The reason is, probably, that the letters
from Montegrano always ask for something, and the emigrant,
whose advantage now lies elsewhere, loses patience with them.
The relative absence of emigration, as well as of gifts from persons who have emigrated, is a significant impediment to economic development. Some Italian towns, whose ethos is different,
have benefited enormously from continuing close ties with
emigrants who have prospered in the New World.[3]

5. *In a society of amoral familists, office-holders, feeling no*

3. McDonald writes in a personal letter: "Since 1927 Italians who are
not officially assisted may be nominated and paid for by relatives or
friends resident here in Australia. Solidarity of some kind is needed for
chains of such emigration to have continued 30 years. Montegrano folk
apparently would not help each other. In Reggio Calabria, community
solidarity is lacking yet there is nuclear family solidarity plus relatively
strong identification with and participation in cliques of certain relatives
selected from the kindred kinship system plus certain friends (especially
compari and *commare*). I have found that these nuclear family-clique
members are the Calabrians who form the links in the migration chains.
Since cliques of relatives and friends overlap in their system, these chains
are snowballing despite the lack of community solidarity. In fact, compar-
ing the rate of growth of Calabrian settlements of the above clique-nuclear
family solidarity type with Calabrian settlements of the Montegrano
solidarity nuclear family type, I have found that the former grew very
much faster than the latter."

identification with the purposes of the organization, will not work harder than is necessary to keep their places or (if such is within the realm of possibility) to earn promotion. Similarly, professional people and educated people generally will lack a sense of mission or calling. Indeed, official position and special training will be regarded by their possessors as weapons to be used against others for private advantage.

In southern Italy, the indifference of the bureaucracy is notorious. "A zealous official is as rare as a white fly," a man who had retired after 49 years in the public service remarked.

"From the President of the Republic down to the last little Italian," a landowner said, "there is a complete lack of any sense of duty—especially of the sense of duty to do productive work."

The schoolteachers of Montegrano notably lack a sense of calling. It is not uncommon for a teacher to come late to class or to miss class altogether. At best the teacher teaches four hours a day and takes no further part in the lives of the children. An engineer from northern Italy was shocked at what he saw in Montegrano. "During the summer vacation," he said, "a teacher in the north may hold informal classes. He will take the children on walks into the country and explain a bit about nature. Or they will go on picnics and sing together. The teacher is a part of the children's lives out of school as well as in." In Montegrano, he found, teachers spend the summer loafing in the *piazza* and they do not speak to their pupils when they see them.

"Study and education," a young teacher who was himself of an artisan family explained, "has helped some people to succeed. It has helped them by giving them an advantage over the ignorant. With their knowledge, they are better able to exploit ignorance. They are able to cheat more dexterously."

With other professionals the situation is more or less the same. The pharmacist, a left-wing socialist who enjoys a government monopoly and is one of the richest men in town, feels himself under no obligation to stock the antibiotics and other new medicines which the doctor prescribes or to extend credit to those desperately in need. The doctor himself, although an outstanding man in many ways, does not feel under an obligation to provide himself with the bare essentials of equipment for modern medical practice.

6. *In a society of amoral familists, the law will be disregarded when there is no reason to fear punishment. Therefore individuals will not enter into agreements which depend upon legal processes for their enforcement unless it is likely that the law will be enforced and unless the cost of securing enforcement will not be so great as to make the undertaking unprofitable.*

This, of course, is another impediment to organization and to economic and other development.

It is taken for granted that all those who can cheat on taxes will do so. Minimum wage laws and laws which require the employer to make social security payments on the wages of domestic servants are universally ignored.

An employer who can get away with it is almost sure to cheat his employees. If the employer is a local man, the worker can get justice by appealing to the Marshal, whose informal powers are great. Otherwise the worker is usually cheated. The new municipal building was built by contractors from Matera who paid Montegrano laborers less than the legal minimum and left town owing several of them wages for their last month's work. Since the employer was not a local man, the Marshal could do nothing. In principle the workers could appeal to a labor commission in Potenza. In practice they had to reconcile themselves to the fact that they had been cheated.

Frequently the worker is prevented by self-interest from taking his case to the Marshal. He cannot afford to be on bad terms with the employer: it is better to be cheated than to be deprived of employment altogether. Accordingly, it is the custom for the employer to pay only at his convenience. A peasant may have to go, hat in hand, to the *signore* month after month to ask politely for the dollar or two that is owed.

Mutual distrust between landlords and tenants accounts in

part for the number of tiny, owner-operated farms in Montegrano. Rather than work a larger unit on shares, an arrangement which would be more profitable but which would necessitate getting along with a landlord, the peasant prefers to go it alone on his uneconomic holding. Twenty-one peasants were asked which they would prefer, to own eight hectares of land or to sharecrop 40. One said he would prefer to sharecrop the larger holding "because even if I had to be under another and to work a little harder, the gain would be much more." None of the others thought the gain from the larger holding would offset the burden of having to get along with a landlord. Their explanations showed how anxiety, suspicion, and hate make cooperation burdensome.[4]

I would prefer to be the owner of eight hectares rather than have the rental of 40 because if you are an owner no one commands you and furthermore you are not always worried that tomorrow your half may not be yours and so always under the necessity of being careful.

✦ ✦ ✦

I would prefer to be the owner of eight hectares or even less than to work someone else's land. I've had experience with that already and it is really unbearable because the owners always think you are stealing from them.

✦ ✦ ✦

4. Seventeen of these peasants were also asked which they would prefer, to own eight hectares or to have a steady job paying 1,000 *lire* a day. Eleven preferred the cash wage; all but one because there would be no worry or uncertainty. Of the six who preferred to own land, two said that their incomes would be greater, two said that they would be independent of an employer, and two said that they would have both larger incomes and independence.

To the peasants, the cash wage of 1,000 *lire* was associated with a "company" such as contracts with public agencies to do road repairs, not with private individuals. The company, the peasant feels, is less likely to cheat and is in general more dependable. One said he would prefer the wage if the employer were a company but the land if the employer were a private party.

I would prefer a little land of my own to renting 40 hectares because, as I have already said, I hate the rich who sit in the breeze all year and come around only when it is time to divide the produce which I have worked hard with so many sacrifices to grow.

7. *The amoral familist who is an office-holder will take bribes when he can get away with it. But whether he takes bribes or not, it will be assumed by the society of amoral familists that he does.*[5]

There is no way of knowing to what extent bribery actually exists in Montegrano. There is abundant evidence, however, that it is widely believed to be common. The peasants are sure

5. An interview with the Communist mayor of Grottole, another village of Lucania, by E. A. Bayne of the American Universities Field Staff, reveals the same selfishness and distrust that are evident in Montegrano.

After explaining to Bayne that the peasants of Grottole would not work together—that all wanted something for themselves—the mayor asked if the Americans would give the village a tractor. After he had been discouraged in this hope, the mayor said,

"When you leave here I will go down in the street with my people, and they will ask me, 'Did you get any help for us?' And I will try to explain that you are not officials—not even rich tourists—but journalists. 'Why then,' they will say, 'have you bought them wine and coffee with our money and now have nothing to show for it?' "

At the conclusion of his interview Bayne laid a few thousand *lire* on the mayor's desk and asked if he would distribute it where it would do the most good. Perhaps there was a Christmas fund for children? The mayor's consternation was immediate. With politeness but with unmistakable firmness he refused.

"You do not understand my people [he protested]. If I were to accept this gift which *I* understand, those people in the street would soon ask if there had not been more and how much I had kept for myself. We have no Christmas fund, for who would contribute to it? . . ."

Two years later Bayne revisited Grottole and found that the mayor had been defeated for re-election and had taken to drink. "He didn't do anything for the people and they became tired of him," someone explained. "Now we have a new mayor—this one is really a fascist. He won't do anything either."

Quoted with permission from American Universities Field Staff letters of December 17, 1954, and February 21, 1957.

that the employment officer gives preference to those who bring him presents. They believe, too, that Mayor Spomo made a fortune by selling the communal forest without competitive bids. Better informed people say that it is highly unlikely that there is graft in the administration of the commune: its affairs are too closely supervised from Potenza. However, many upper class people agree that bribery and favoritism are widespread in southern Italy at large. A teacher said,

Today one gets ahead only by bribes and recommendations. All of the examinations are infected with this disease and those who get ahead are the ones with the most drag. To me this is odious. I would do anything not to have to see it.

The principal merchant is building a cinema. Before it goes into operation he must have a permit from the proper authority. After months of waiting, his request for a permit had not been acted upon. "If I took an envelope with $160 and slipped it into the right pocket, I would have my permission right away," he told an interviewer. "It's the little yellow envelope that gets things done. Big and small, they all take bribes."

"Why don't you do it, then?"

"Because I don't have $160 to spare."

8. *In a society of amoral familists the weak will favor a regime which will maintain order with a strong hand.*

Until it involved them in war, Fascism appealed to many peasants—at least so they now say—because by enforcing the laws rigorously, it protected them. Here are some answers given by peasants to the question, "What did the Fascists claim to stand for?"

The Fascists said they wanted to be commanders of all. We had no free speech under them, but Mussolini was a good administrator. The Fascists were very bad, but you could send a child any distance unmolested when they were in power. Now you have to walk with a hand on your pocket and a hand on your hat to keep from being robbed.

✦   ✦   ✦

The Fascists wanted the peasants to have a better life. There was an eight-hour day and a standard rate of pay. It was a published rate. If a proprietor made you work ten hours you went to the employment office and they would force him to pay the right wage. Now it is everyone for himself, and everyone tries to get the most work for the least pay out of the peasant.

⚡ ⚡ ⚡

I don't know what they wanted, but they did make severe laws. There was order and you had rights and duties. You had the right to be paid when you worked and it was a duty to pay workers for work done. They looked after the children too. There were subsidies for large families and help when a new baby was born. Nowadays there is supposed to be help, but it is not enforced.

⚡ ⚡ ⚡

I do not remember what it was the Fascists wanted. I only remember that in those days one made out better than today. In those days the worker was well off and not unhappy. Also there were many more aids. Instead, today, nobody cares. If it were during the days of Fascism, the things that happen now would not happen. Today a worker must wait to be paid . . . must wait for the convenience of his employer. Many times months pass without his being paid. During Fascism, this would never have happened.

A landowner made a similar explanation:

During Fascism, parents were really forced to send their children to school. There could be no excuses, like lack of clothes or books, because the government really provided those where necessary. There was an official who stood outside the school building each morning at 8:30. He gave the children bread and cheese or marmalade and the children would go into the school to eat. School would begin at nine. Now if ten suits are sent to the commune for the children, we are lucky if a cuff of one suit really gets here . . . it just melts by the wayside. The laws are all there, but no one enforces them.

A merchant argued that the consumer was better off under Fascist regulation than under present-day competition. "Cloth was grade-labelled and marked with a fixed price along the selvedge. Everything was controlled. You knew what you were getting for your money. Now, unless you really understand cloth, a merchant can sell you inferior material at high prices. It was good for the customer and good for the merchant too. The customer knew what he was getting and the merchant could count on his twenty or thirty percent. Some people get one hundred percent today."

A teacher had this recollection of Fascism:

During Fascism there was a great spirit of emulation among the pupils and good discipline. Today all this is gone; children grow up very rude and the teacher in school must always have a stick in hand because the children are fighting among themselves all of the time.

9. *In a society of amoral familists, the claim of any person or institution to be inspired by zeal for public rather than private advantage will be regarded as fraud.*

A young man said,

If I decided that I wanted to do something for Montegrano, I would enter my name on the list at election time, and everyone would ask, 'Why does he want to be mayor?' If ever anyone wants to do anything, the question always is: what is he after?

Anti-clericalism is widespread in Montegrano, and the usual objection to priests is that they are "money grubbers" and hypocrites." In fact, the priests seem to be no more concerned with gain than are other professionals, and their level of living is no higher than that of the others. They are peculiarly liable to attack, however, because the church professes to be unselfish.

Socialists and Communists, like priests, are liable to be regarded as pious frauds. "There are socialists of the mouth and socialists of the heart," a peasant woman explained.

The extraordinary bitterness and, as it seems to an outsider, unfairness with which so many peasants accuse others of hypocrisy is to be understood, in part, perhaps, as an expression of guilt feelings. As is explained elsewhere, the peasant is not unaware that charity is a virtue. Not practicing it himself, he feels some guilt therefore, and he projects this as hostility against those institutions, especially the church, which preach the virtue of charity and through which, perhaps, he would like to be vicariously virtuous.

10. *In the society of amoral familists there will be no connection between abstract political principle (i.e., ideology) and concrete behavior in the ordinary relationships of every day life.*

In Montegrano, the principle left-wing socialists are the doctor and the pharmacist, two of the town's most prosperous gentlemen. The doctor, although he has called upon the government to provide a hospital, has not arranged an emergency room or even equipped his own office. The pharmacist, a government-licensed monopolist, gives an absolute minimum of service at extremely high prices (Signora Prato paid five cents for a single aspirin tablet!) and is wholly unconcerned with local affairs, i.e., those which would have implications for action by him.

The discrepancy between ideology and behavior in practical affairs tends to discredit ideology in the eyes of the peasants. Prato was one of those who assembled in the *piazza* when Dr. Gino tried to organize a branch of the Socialist Party.

I went a few times and it all sounded very good [he said later]. But that Spring Don Franco hired a mule to cultivate his vineyard, and I thought to myself, What can this be? What can Socialism mean? Why does Don Franco, who is such a believer in it, hire a mule instead of the ten workers he used to hire? There are ten people out of work. And it wouldn't cost him any more to use them than to use the mule.

What ignorance! [the doctor exclaimed when he was told what Prato said]. Cultivation well done by hand is better than cultivation done with a mule. But the workers here must be watched all the time because they don't really know their jobs, and it is a nuisance to have to be on hand to keep watch. With a mule, you can at least see that the whole row has been done the same way.

11. *In a society of amoral familists there will be no leaders and no followers. No one will take the initiative in outlining a course of action and persuading others to embark upon it (except as it may be to his private advantage to do so) and, if one did offer leadership, the group would refuse it out of distrust.*

Apparently there has never been in Montegrano a peasant leader to other peasants. Objectively, there is a basis for such leadership to develop: the workers on road gangs, for example, share grievances and one would expect them to develop feelings of solidarity.

Suspicion of the would-be leader probably reduces the effectiveness of the doctor, the midwife, and the agricultural agent as teachers. When a peasant was asked whether she could get birth control information from the midwife, she replied, "Of course not. It is not to her interest that I limit the size of my family."

The nearest approximation to leadership is the patron-client relationship. By doing small favors (e.g., by lending a few bushels of grain during the winter, by giving cast-off clothing, or by taking a child from a large family as a housemaid), a well-to-do person may accumulate a clientele of persons who owe him return favors and, of course, deference. Such clients constitute a "following," perhaps, but the patron is not a "leader" in any significant sense. In Montegrano, moreover, none of the well-to-do has troubled to develop much of a clientele. One reason is, perhaps, that the leading families are not engaged in factionable squabbles, and so the advantage to be had from a clientele does not outweigh the expense and inconvenience of maintaining it.

12. *The amoral familist will use his ballot to secure the greatest material gain in the short run. Although he may have decided views as to his long-run interest, his class interest, or the public interest, these will not effect his vote if the family's short-run, material advantage is in any way involved.*

Prato, for example, is a monarchist as a matter of principle: he was born and brought up one and he believes that monarchy is best because Italy is too poor to afford frequent elections. These principles do not affect his vote, however. "Before elections," he explains, "all the parties send people around who say, 'Vote for our party.' We always say 'Yes,' but when we go to vote, we vote for the party we think has given us the most." The Christian Democratic party has given Prato a few days work on the roads each year. Therefore he votes for it. If it ceased to give him work and if there were no advantage to be had from voting for another party, he would be a monarchist again. If Mayor Spomo has influence with the Minister of Agriculture, he should be kept despite his haughtiness and his stealing. But if Councilmen Viva and Lasso can get a larger project than the mayor can get, or if they can get one quicker, then down with him.

13. *The amoral familist will value gains accruing to the community only insofar as he and his are likely to share them. In fact, he will vote against measures which will help the community without helping him because, even though his position is unchanged in absolute terms, he considers himself worse off if his neighbors' position changes for the better. Thus it may happen that measures which are of decided general benefit will provoke a protest vote from those who feel that they have not shared in them or have not shared in them sufficiently.*

In 1954, the Christian Democratic party showed the voters of Basso that vast sums had been spent on local public works. Nevertheless the vote went to the Communists. There are other reasons which help to account for the vote (the Christian Democratic candidate was a merchant who would not give credit and was cordially disliked and distrusted), but it seems likely that the very effectiveness of the Christian Democratic propaganda may have helped to cause its defeat. Seeing what vast sums had been expended, the voters asked themselves: Who got it all? Why didn't they give me my fair share?

No amoral familist ever gets what he regards as his fair share.

14. *In a society of amoral familists the voter will place little*

*confidence in the promises of the parties. He will be apt to use
his ballot to pay for favors already received (assuming, of
course, that more are in prospect) rather than for favors which
are merely promised.*

Thus Prato, in the statement quoted above, attaches weight
to past performance rather than to promises. "All the parties
make promises," he says. "The Christian Democratic party had
a chance and it has done a great deal. Why change?" And thus
the writer of the letter quoted in Chapter One, after describing
the enthusiasm with which the new mayor was received after
Spomo's defeat, remarks significantly, "We will wait and see."

The principle of paying for favors received rather than for
ones merely promised gives a great advantage to the party in
power, of course. Its effect, however, is often more than offset
by another principle, as follows:

15. *In a society of amoral familists it will be assumed that
whatever group is in power is self-serving and corrupt. Hardly
will an election be over before the voters will conclude that the
new officials are enriching themselves at their expense and that
they have no intention of keeping the promises they have made.
Consequently, the self-serving voter will use his ballot to pay
the incumbents not for benefits but for injuries, i.e., he will use
it to administer punishment.*

Even though he has more to gain from it than from any
other, the voter may punish a party if he is confident that it
will be elected despite his vote. The ballot being secret, he can
indulge his taste for revenge (or justice) without incurring
losses. (Of course there is some danger that too many will
calculate in this way, and that the election will therefore be lost
by error.)

Addo's switch from Christian Democrat to Communist and
back again to Christian Democrat is to be explained in this way.
The priest in Addo was slightly mad. Some of his eccentricities
nobody minded (he arrayed himself as a cardinal and required
a chicken as part payment for a marriage), but when he left
town a few days before the election taking with him the *pasta,*

sugar, and other election-day presents that had been sent them from the Vatican, the voters of Addo were outraged. Afterward, a new priest soon made matters right.

16. *Despite the willingness of voters to sell their votes, there will be no strong or stable political machines in a society of amoral familists.* *This will be true for at least three reasons: (a) the ballot being secret, the amoral voter cannot be depended upon to vote as he has been paid to vote; (b) there will not be enough short-run material gain from a machine to attract investment in it; and (c) for reasons explained above, it will be difficult to maintain formal organization of any kind whatever.*

Prato says "Yes" to all who ask for his vote. Since they cannot trust him to vote as he promises, none of the parties will offer to buy his vote. The *pasta* and sugar that are distributed by the parties are good-will offerings rather than bribes. The amounts given are, of course, trivial in comparison to what would be paid if there were some way of enforcing the contract.

17. *In a society of amoral familists, party workers will sell their services to the highest bidders. Their tendency to change sides will make for sudden shifts in strength of the parties at the polls.*[6]

6. That voter behavior in the Montegrano district is closely similar to that in much of rural Italy is suggested by the data in an undated report by the Office of Intelligence Research, based on data secured by International Research Associates, Inc., of New York, which includes "profiles" of the political situation in 76 communes ranging in size from 200 to 7,000 electors and located in all parts of Italy. The communes described are those in which Communism made its greatest gains or suffered its greatest losses in the 1953 elections. The data was gathered in field interviews in which citizens were asked to explain the voting shift in their communes. The report shows that local economic issues were by far the most important cause of the voting shifts. Economic doctrine, it shows, was of little importance. National issues—e.g., monarchy, the church, foreign policy—were of even less importance. "Next to economic causes," the report says, "significant changes in the voting pattern appear to have been caused by corruption, graft, injustice (real or fancied), and failure to fulfill promises."

The sudden conversion of the secretary of the Montegrano branch of the Monarchist Party to Communist occurred because Monarchist headquarters in Naples was slow in paying him for his services. When he turned Communist, the Monarchists made a settlement. He then returned to his duties as if nothing had happened.

6

Ethos in Practice

THE value of the hypothesis offered at the beginning of the
last chapter does not depend upon the possibility of showing
that all, or even any, of the people of Montegrano consciously
follow the rule of action set forth there. For the hypothesis to
be useful, it need only be shown that they act *as if* they follow
the rule.[1]

In fact, however, insofar as it is not habitual, behavior in
Montegrano is based upon sentiments, values, beliefs, and ideas
which are consistent with the rule and which can be reduced
to it. In this chapter, these elements of the ethos will be described as they enter into the behavior of the Montegranesi.
But, of course, in Montegrano, as everywhere else, there is some
discrepancy between "real" and "ideal" behavior—between "is"
and "ought." In the next chapter the description of sentiments,
values, beliefs, and ideas will continue, but there the emphasis
will be upon ethos as a set of standards which have little relation to practice.

The individual's attachment to the family must be the starting place for an account of the Montegrano ethos. In fact, an
adult hardly may be said to have an individuality apart from
the family: he exists not as "ego" but as "parent." In most of

1. The methodological point involved here is discussed by Milton
Friedman in *Essays in Positive Economics*, University of Chicago Press,
1953, p. 19.

the 320 stories told by 16 peasants who were given Thematic Apperception Tests,[2] the central character was explicitly, and from the standpoint of the plot usually gratuitously, defined as a father or mother, son or daughter. Just as fairy stories begin, "Once upon a time there was a king . . ." so in Montegrano TAT stories begin "Once upon a time there was a father . . ." If the storyteller wishes to create strong sympathy for his character, he describes him as a poor man who has many children and works hard to support them, or, if the character is a woman, as a poor widow with only one child.

The family consists of father, mother, and their unmarried children. There are relatives, of course, but they are not part of the family in the strict (and therefore narrow) sense.

The adult individual, then, is thought of as a parent bringing up children. In Montegrano this is viewed as—and is in fact—a hard and unremitting struggle. Parents must work desperately merely to keep the family alive. But they have an obligation also to "set the children on the right road," i.e., to put them in a position to marry and have children of their own. This necessitates continued "sacrifices" for the sake of the children. ("There was a poor man who had many children and who made many sacrifices to set them on the right road . . ." TAT stories characteristically begin.) Children are naturally lazy and wayward; all the homilies, scoldings, and beatings an indulgent parent gives them may not suffice to set them on the right road. Parents, therefore, must struggle to overcome their children's natural instability. ("This poor man had a son who paid no attention to his father's advice . . .")

Geppetto's struggles to set Pinocchio upon the right road typify what is for the Montegranesi a fundamental and universal preoccupation.[3]

2. See footnote 10, Chapter Three, p. 61.

3. The author of the Pinocchio story was a northern Italian and what has been said of the Montegrano ethos so far seems to apply to the north no less than the south. Ten peasants in the province of Rovigo (region of Veneto) who were given the same TAT showed a similar, although less marked, tendency to see every situation in terms of family.

No matter how hard the parents struggle, the family may suddenly be destroyed or reduced to beggary. The peasant expects some dreadful calamity to befall it at any moment. In his view a mountain of woe hangs over it by a slender thread. Ninety percent of the TAT stories told by Montegrano people had themes of calamity or misfortune; in some stories the calamities and misfortunes were averted; in many more they were not. Only two or three of the 320 stories were positively happy in tone.

Table 3—TAT Stories Having Themes of Calamity or Misfortune

	Southern Italy[1]	Northern Italy[2]	Rural Kansas[3]
a. Calamity; story ends in death, insanity, or blighting of all hope.	44	13	9
b. Misfortune; story ends with injury of "hero," loss of money, death of live-stock, etc.	20	11	7
c. Calamity or misfortune averted or mitigated; story deals with an escape, fears that prove unfounded, tribulation followed by eventual success or alleviation.	26	38	26
d. Safety; the story is not necessarily happy but there is no theme of peril.	7	29	50
e. Unclassifiable; fragmentary or purely descriptive	3	9	8
ALL	100	100	100

1. 320 stories by 16 persons (seven married couples and two youths) in Montegrano; all laborers. Complete Murray test of each respondent.

2. 200 stories by 10 persons (five married couples) in the province of Rovigo (bounded by Verona, Padova, and Venice); all laborers. Complete Murray test of each respondent.

3. 386 stories by 30 persons (15 married couples) in Vinland, Kansas; farm owners. The following Murray cards: 1, 2, 3BM and GF, 4, 5, 6BM and GF, 10, 11, 13, 16, 18BM and GF, 19 and 20.

Here, for example, is the "picture" which Prato's wife "saw" on a blank card. All Montegrano people who were tested told some similar stories ending in death and disaster.

A woman is watching a dead child with grief. There was a family —very poor—which lived by the work and sacrifice of the parents.

They had only one child and consequently loved him immensely and for him made all of the sacrifices. But one day he fell ill. They believed it was nothing, but instead the illness did not pass and in fact became worse. In order to save him, the parents spent the little they had, but the doctors were useless. After five or six months of illness he died, leaving the parents in pain and misery.

Normal people in other cultures when given the same test do not show themselves so preoccupied with calamity. In the following table, the responses of the Montegranesi are compared with those of farm laborers in the Rovigo region of northern Italy and with those of farm people in Kansas. All the 16 Montegranesi tested told stories ending in calamity and the average number of such stories told was 8.7. Of 10 northerners, nine told an average of 2.9 such stories. Of 30 rural Kansans, only 19 told stories ending in calamity, and the average number of such stories told by them was only 1.5.

The people of Montegrano are aware of their extreme apprehensiveness and even have a name for it. *Preoccupazione* is a state of mingled worry, fear, anxiety, and foreboding. One may be *preoccupato* with regard to some particular matter, even one of not much importance. But the word is most often

Table 4—TAT Stories Ending in Death, by Cause of Calamity

	PERCENT OF ALL STORIES ENDING IN CALAMITY	
Cause of Calamity	Southern Italian—%	Northern Italian—%
A. The Natural Order		
1. Illness and other natural causes	33	7
2. War	9	7
3. Mischance (hunting, accident, attack by animal, etc.)	24	16
All	66	30
B. Act of Man		
4. Malevolent or criminal act	17	35
5. Act promoted by love or lust; infidelity	13	31
ALL	30	66
C. Unclassifiable	4	4
Total	100	100
	(136 stories)	(26 stories)

used to refer to chronic, diffuse fear for the welfare of the family. What if a storm should destroy the crops? Or if one or both of the parents should die? The peasant thinks that the heavy burden of worry he bears is a defining characteristic of his class. But actually the gentleman is also *preoccupato*. What will happen to his family if he cannot find dowries for his daughters?

As Table 4 shows, the Montegrano peasant seems to fear nature more than man. The fear of death from natural causes is particularly strong in him. So few stories ending in calamity were told by northerners that little significance can be attached to this part of the tabulation; so far as the evidence goes, however, it suggests that the northerners think calamity is more likely to come from man than from nature.

*   *   *

In such a fearful world a parent cannot count on achieving anything by his own effort and enterprise. The conditions and means of success are all beyond his control. He may struggle to get ahead, but in the end he will probably be crushed by the insane fury of events. Here, for example, is the story which Paolo told about a blank card:

This picture shows a lovely house with a garden and small fountain in front. There was a man who with much effort and many sacrifices succeeded in making a small pile. He bought a bit of land and at the same time continued to work hard and to profit. Then with many sacrifices he succeeded in building the house, very beauteous and commodious. But he was not able to enjoy it because just as it was being finished he unexpectedly died.

Some—but by no means all—of the Montegranesi look to the saints and to God to ward off calamity. A peasant woman whose life consists of a daily walk down a country lane to her field and back again thanks God for His mercy in aiding her to make the trip in safety:

Every morning when I wake up I thank God for having brought us to a new day, and at night when I come back from the country with the goat and the pig and the lamb and the children, I go to bed and I thank God that he has brought us to the end of another day . . . that the day is over and without harm.

Only the intervention of God, the believer thinks, will restrain the mad fury of events, establish a few moments of order and predictability, and so set up the conditions under which successful effort becomes possible. When Pasqualina starts the day, she says, "Christ, open the door for me this day." She says this because she has few means and must therefore depend upon God's help. She knows that He is aware of her condition and that, in fact, her condition is the result of His will. Whatever happens, she is in God's hands. Nothing comes to her without God's help:

This year we planted three *tomoli* and we expected to get fourteen or fifteen. We got five. But every year we go on planting, trusting that God will not turn his back on us. And so we go on every year, hoping for the best and for His help.

When God wards off calamity, ability and initiative count for something. Pasquale and his wife buy fertilizer every year "so that if Christ should give us a good year we would have done our part." But since one cannot know in advance whether God will intervene or not, life is no less a gamble than if He did not exist or never intervened. "Whatever we have comes from Christ," Pasquale says, adding in the next breath, "In spite of all, we are always beaten to the ground." Gambling that Christ might favor them, he and his wife have bought fertilizer year after year and now they are deeply in debt.

Many of the Montegranesi are not religious. God exists, no doubt, and it would be unseemly not to pay Him respect. But there is no use trying to gain His protection or favor by right behavior or even by worship,[4] God is like luck, and if luck could be managed by intention, it would not be luck.[5]

4. When he sows the first handful of wheat, Prato says, "In the name of God." With the last handful he says, "Grow! Grow!" If there is a dry spell the priest prays for rain. With the first cut of the sickle, Prato says, "In the name of God." In his opinion, however, these formulae have

Great success, then, is obtained by the favor of the saints or by luck, certainly not by thrift, work, and enterprise. These may be important if one is already lucky, but not otherwise, and few would invest large amounts of effort—any more than they would invest large amounts of fertilizer—on the rather remote possibility of good fortune.[6]

The idea that one's welfare depends crucially upon conditions beyond one's control—upon luck or the caprice of a saint—and that one can at best only improve upon good fortune, not create it—this idea must certainly be a check on initiative. Its influence on economic life is obvious: one who lives in so capricious a world is not likely to save and invest in the expectation of ultimate gain. In politics, too, it must have an effect. Where everything depends upon luck or Divine intervention, there is no point in community action. The community, like the individual, may hope or pray, but it is not likely to take its destiny into its own hands.

✓   ✓   ✓

In the Montegrano view, the conditions of life—the brutal and senseless conditions of life—determine how men will be-

---

nothing to do with the success of the harvest: "When the air is the right temperature it rains, prayer or no prayer." He counts himself a religious man, nevertheless, and thinks it is a good thing to pray even though praying makes no practical difference.

5. "In Calabria," McDonald comments in a personal communication, "ritual is a way of earning supernatural patronage and a favorable course of events. However, since the moral side of Christianity is not stressed and there is no measuring rod for predicting one's worthiness (priests are not held to be sure arbiters and exemplars of behavior), there can be little confidence in the usefulness of ritual for attaining grace and good fortune."

6. Compare this with the Calvinist view described by Max Weber, in *op. cit.*, p. 109: ". . . the wonderfully purposeful organization and arrangement of this cosmos is, according both to the revelation of the Bible and to natural intuition, evidently designed by God to serve the utility of the human race. *This makes labour in the service of impersonal social usefulness appear to promote the glory of God and hence to be willed by Him.*" [Italics added.]

have. In so fearful a world, a parent must do all he can to protect his family. He must preoccupy himself exclusively with its *interesse*. The *interesse* of the family is its material, short-run advantage.[7] The tireless and cunning pursuit of advantage cannot be depended upon to secure the welfare of the family: the threat of calamity hangs over all, even the unsleeping. But, little as it may count against the overwhelming uncertainties of the universe, the pursuit of *interesse* is at least something—perhaps the only thing—the individual can do to give a measure of protection to his family.

In the Montegrano mind, any advantage that may be given to another is necessarily at the expense of one's own family.[8] Therefore, one cannot afford the luxury of charity, which is giving others more than their due, or even of justice, which is giving them their due. The world being what it is, all those

7. The word *interesse* has the same meanings as the English word "interest," viz., both "advantage" and "excitement of feeling or attention." However, among the peasants of Montegrano, it is used in the first sense only. An interview schedule asked, "What is the farthest you have ever been from Montegrano?" and then, "What interested you most there?" The reply to the second question was always either an explanation of why it was to the individual's advantage to go there or of how he happened to go there without having any reason of advantage (e.g., military service).

8. Norman Douglas was struck by this in Calabria forty years ago. "Here life is give and take, and lucky he who takes more than he gives; it is what Professor Mahaffy calls the ingrained selfishness of the Greek character. Speaking of all below the upper classes, I should say that disinterested benevolence is apt to surpass their comprehension, a good-natured person being regarded as weak in the head. Has this man, then, no family, that he should benefit strangers? Or is he one of nature's unfortunates—soft-witted? Thus they argue. They will do acts of spontaneous kindness towards their family, far oftener than is customary with us. But outside the narrow sphere, *interesse* (Odyssean self-advantage) is the mainspring of their actions. Whence their smooth and glozing manners towards the stranger, and those protestations of undying affection which beguile the unwary—they wish to be forever in your good graces, for sooner or later you may be of use; and if perchance you do content them, they will marvel (philosophically) at your grotesque generosity, your lack of discrimination and restraint." *Old Calabria*, Houghton Mifflin Co., New York, 1915, p. 124.

who stand outside of the small circle of the family are at least potential competitors and therefore also potential enemies. Toward those who are not of the family the reasonable attitude is suspicion. The parent knows that other families will envy and fear the success of his family and that they are likely to seek to do it injury. He must therefore fear them and be ready to do them injury in order that they may have less power to injure him and his.

Even within the family solidarity is not complete or symmetrical. Until they are ready for marriage, the children are expected to subordinate their wishes to the *interesse* of the family. Prato, for example, had to give up learning the shoemaker's trade after two years apprenticeship in order to earn money for his sister's dowry; from the standpoint of the family, it was more important that she make a good marriage than that he become an artisan. The claims of the family on the child weaken as it approaches adulthood, however, and by the time of marriage he or she is preoccupied with the *interesse* of the family of procreation which is in prospect and ready to subordinate that of the old family of orientation to it. Thus Maria Prato, telling of the accidental strangulation of her younger brother's lamb, made it clear that her *interesse* was not identical with that of her father, mother, and brother:

It was Giovanni's lamb, and he felt so bad he lay down by it and cried all night. My father cried too. We all did. Even I, because we might have used it for the *festa* when I get married.

Marriages are normally for *interesse* and, until the vows have been said, there is profound distrust on both sides of the bargain. Here is Prato's account of his courtship:

In 1935 I was old enough to marry. My sisters wanted me to take a wife because they had no time to do services for me.

At that time there was a law that anyone who was 25 years old and not married had to pay a "celibacy" tax of 125 *lire*. That amount was much, if we recall that to earn it you had to work 25 days. I thought it over and finally decided to marry.

My present wife was at that time working with relatives of my employer. Once I stopped her and asked her to marry me, and she liked the idea too, but I had to tell it before her father. He was happy to accept me, and we talked about what she had to bring [as dowry] and what I had to do.

He asked me to bring my mother to call so that everything would be fine. The next time I brought my mother, and we had a nice feast. When I wanted to meet my fiancée I had to ask the boss' permission.

In 1937 I asked the girl and her family to hasten the marriage before I was 25 years old. The father told me that she was not ready with the dowry. I asked him if at least we couldn't have the civil marriage performed so as to escape the tax. We performed the civil ceremony on February 6, 1938, two months late, so that I had to pay the tax for that year.

Once my mother and I went to Addo to visit my father-in-law in order to discuss and establish definitely what they were going to give us [in the dowry]. My mother wanted everything to be conveyed through a notary. My father-in-law gave us one *tomolo* of land and my mother gave the little house, but she reserved for herself the right to use it. Everything was written on official tax-stamp paper by the notary. As soon as my wife was ready with the dowry the church marriage was set for August 25, 1938.

At the time a new family is established, attachments to the old ones weaken. The wedding arrangements provide opportunities for the bride and groom to get on bad terms with their in-laws. Prato's autobiography continues:

Before that I went to visit my father-in-law to make plans for the wedding party and for getting from one town to another. My wife's mother was dead and she had a step-mother. The step-mother was haughty and she asked me how I was going to bring the daughter from Addo to Montegrano. I said, "I will hire one car and you get another so we can go to Montegrano." But she scoffed.

I went to Addo with a car on the day set, and we got married in the church. After that my wife and I got in the car and so did some other people. My parents-in-law were left out and they were angry with me. But it was not my fault; they could have taken another car.

When a man marries he often ceases to be on good terms with a parent, brothers or sisters, or with his whole paternal family. Before his marriage Prato gave his earnings to his mother to help provide a dowry for a half-sister. Afterward he and the half-sister were on the worst possible terms and for a long time he did not speak to his mother.

Ill will serves the useful function of protecting the new family against demands that might be made upon it by the old. But it also prevents cooperation among members of the family.[9] The division of land into tiny, widely scattered parcels occurs partly because of family squabbles. For example, Prato's half-sister owns a patch of land next to his. She cannot work it herself, but she will not sell or rent it to him, and consequently it lies idle. If peasants were generally on good terms with their siblings, it might be possible in some cases to rationalize the distribution of land by a series of exchanges.

Even when there is no falling out between them, the son's attachment to his parents all but dissolves when he marries. Once he has a wife and children of his own, it is not expected that he will concern himself with the welfare of his parents, unless, perhaps, they are nearly starving. As a laborer explained,

My family never did anything for me and I never did anything for any of them. If they happen to be at my house and there is bread I offer them some. If I go to their house and there is bread they offer it to me. I am too poor to be doing anything for anyone.

No such problem of relationship arises with uncles, aunts, cousins, and more distant relatives. They are not in a position to make demands and so there is no special need for protection against them. One is on a more intimate basis with them than

9. In his study of a peasant community near Rome, Donald S. Pitkin remarks that relatives (*parenti*) "do not constitute an isolated unit and rarely act collectively, not only for situational considerations but for one reason or another members of one's kindred may be at odds with each other. A case in point is that of five middle-aged siblings, four sisters and a brother. One of the sisters is on speaking terms with the brother alone, so that for her children, relationships with their four aunts and cousins are more restricted than they would be ordinarily." *Land Tenure and Family Organization in an Italian Village*, Ph.D. dissertation, Harvard University, 1954, p. 194.

with non-relatives, but in the usual case an uncle or cousin would not enter a house uninvited, and a peasant would not leave a key with a relative when going to the fields.

In principle there is a close and unbreakable bond between the individual and his godparents (*compare* and *comare*): those who stand with one at the altar become spiritual parents and—in principle—one must love and revere them under all circumstances. According to peasant opinion, one's godfather and godmother ought to be regarded, and to regard themselves, as "second parents." In fact, however, they are not expected to do more than take a friendly interest in the godchild, offer him good counsel, and, if they can afford to, make him a small gift at Christmas and at Easter. The godchild, for his part, addresses them with particular respect and brings them gifts on the holidays. It is bad form to have unpleasantness with one's *compare* or *comare*, but this does not always prevent one or both parties from predatory acts against the other. Prato's autobiography, for example, includes this passage:

At this time there was no work, taxes had to be paid, and my family was growing. Once my *compare* asked me if I wanted to go work for him as a year-round hand. I was very glad to do so, and we agreed that he was to pay me three *quintals* of grain a year, 1,000 *lire* a month, and my food. He promised that since my family was growing he would give me the "family allowance." A year passed and I didn't see the allowance. He kept telling me it was the fault of the Social Security Office.

In such a case as this, many—but by no means all—Montegranesi would submit to being cheated rather than go to law with a godparent. In fact, in selecting godparents, peasants take pains to find someone with whom they are not likely to have business relations. To have a *compare* with whom one cannot in decency go to law may put one, as Prato discovered, at a disadvantage. (It is an interesting sidelight on family relations that for this reason one does not choose a godparent from among close relatives: it is taken for granted that one is likely to have lawsuits or other unpleasantness with them.)

Friends are luxuries that the Montegranesi feel they cannot afford. Prato, for example, pairs off with a certain man when they work on the same job, but he does not see this man off the job and he does not consider him a special friend. What visiting the Pratos do is with the parents of their prospective son-in-law, and these visits take place only on special occasions like Easter. All of the peasants who were asked said that they have no special friends but that they "get along with everybody."

Peasants sometimes exchange labor or make each other small loans of bread or cash, but they do so from self-intterest, not from charity or fellow-feeling. No one expects help from another if the other stands to lose by helping. The peasant who works for another keeps a careful record of his hours. Even trivial favors create an obligation and must be repaid. When a visiting social scientist said he planned to leave the key to his house with a neighbor for a few days while he was away, his landlord pointed out that such a thing would be foolish. "You would needlessly create an obligation which you would have to repay."

As the Montegranesi see it, friends and neighbors are not only potentially costly but potentially dangerous as well. No family, they think, can stand to see another prosper without feeling envy and wishing the other harm. Friends and neighbors are, of course, peculiarly liable to envy, both because they know more about one's business than do others and because they feel themselves to be more directly in competition.

The apprehensions people have of what may come from too close attachments to friends and neighbors are suggested by the following TAT stories:

There were two fathers of families who loved each other very much and always worked together for the welfare of their families. One day there was some wage work and they planned together how they could get it. They succeeded and the work began very well but then between the two of them jealousy began to grow so much that in the end they hated each other and finally one day one of them killed the other and the two families were left in their misery. (7BM)

※ ※ ※

There was a poor man who had absolutely nothing and found himself in great misery. One day someone gave him two pigeons and he, instead of eating them, tried to raise them and, in fact, he raised them very well. He became the subject of envy when he had reached this happy state. And one of the envious ones one day poisoned a little grain and threw it to all the pigeons who all died, leaving the poor man in his misery as before. (19)

※ ※ ※

There was a widow who had five children. In order to support them she succeeded in finding a job in a bakery. So with this labor things went well. Some of the neighbors, however, had a great envy for this woman and, in fact, they ruined her. One day while she was a little distance from the ovens somebody threw some poison into the dough so that many persons who ate the bread became ill. And it was decided that the woman had done this. She was thrown out of the bake shop, put in jail, and had to leave her children on the street. (17GF)

One can protect one's family from the envy of friends by not having any. But one cannot avoid having neighbors. Moreover, there is always the possibility that one may have an urgent need of them—the house may catch on fire or it may be necessary for someone to run for the midwife. Accordingly, relations among neighbors are generally good. (That it is the need neighbors have of each other which makes relations good is seen from the fact that when one moves into another part of town the ex-neighbors soon cease to greet each other when they meet on the street.) However, one takes the precaution of tempting one's neighbors as little as possible: a piece of sausage or an egg is carried home under the apron so that they will not see it and become envious.

Being a fellow-townsman (*paesano*) is not an important tie except possibly when outsiders are involved. The tie, in any case, is based more upon self-interest than upon any sense of

obligation: a fellow-townsman is a person who one is sure to
see many times again, a sufficient reason for treating him differ-
ently than others. Maria Prato bought a sewing machine from
a woman who was leaving Montegrano to live in Rome. The
machine turned out to be defective, and Maria lost what was
for her a large sum. "Since we are *paesani*," she said indig-
nantly, "she should have spoken clearly to me. She should have
said, 'The machine has this defect.' She knew of the defect and
was able to hide it when she demonstrated the machine in her
house. If it had been I who was selling the machine I would
have said, 'We are *paesani*. This machine is not for you.' And
I would have sold it to an outsider (*forestière*)." Maria's understanding of the conventions was correct, but she left out of
account the fact that the woman who was moving would not
have to suffer the normal consequences of acting unconven-
tionally, i.e., she would not encounter Maria or the other
townspeople again.[10]

Aside from the need to protect his family from envy and
from claims on its resources, the Montegranese has a strong
reason to avoid close attachments. He is afraid that his women
may be seduced. He does not permit a companion to get on
familiar terms with his household because he would take advantage of his first opportunity. So would a relative or a godfather. "Keep the closest watch on cousins and godfathers," is
the protective male's maxim.

✦ ✦ ✦

10. When Paolo heard of Maria's misfortune he said that he himself
had sold a machine of the same model and with the same defect to someone from Basso. "It was wrong for that woman to sell the machine to
Maria," he remarked.

"But why did you sell a defective machine to a woman of Basso?" he
was asked by the visiting social scientist.

"Because," he explained patiently, "the *forestière* buys it and goes off.
It is his problem after that. But if I sell it to a *paesano*, what can I do?
I see him every day. It would not be good."

"But is it right to steal from a *forestière*?" the social scientist persisted.

"Ah," said Paolo, "That is not stealing. He tries to gyp me and I try
to gyp him. It is a different matter altogether. *È un imbroglio.*"

Among the gentry self-interest is not universally material advantage in the short-run. A few gentlemen would probably be willing to make some sacrifice of material goods to obtain prestige, public recognition, "glory." Under the right circumstances this motivation might be politically important. At present it is not, for in Montegrano there are no opportunities to obtain glory in any manner whatever. At present then, the gentry are as exclusively preoccupied with material advantage as are the peasants, and so it is approximately correct to say that amoral familism is the ethos of the whole society—of the upper class as well as of the lower.[11]

There are, however, some important differences in the strategies open to the various classes for the expression of the common ethos. Artisans, merchants, clerks, landowners, and professionals all have opportunities of one kind or another to take the offensive against each other and against the peasant; they are "exploiters" because they have the possibility of being such. The peasant, especially the landless one, is altogether without power. As one of them said sadly, "Only the peasant has no one from whom he can steal." He is restricted by necessity to the use of defensive weapons, especially stubborness, suspicion, secrecy, and lying.

As a rule, however, both in Montegrano and among intellectuals who write about southern Italian society, differences in style of behavior are seen not as variations on a single theme but as altogether distinct characters, characters which are formed by class position.

The peasant lays great stress on class differences and imagines that the upper class is a conspiracy against him. Obviously, he thinks, there are differences of *interesse* between rich and poor. It follows that the rich will be quick to pursue their *interesse* and that in doing so they will exploit the poor; to his

11. McDonald comments that in Calabria "homogeneous values are shared by all classes; differences of behavior between the classes are more a function of the distribution of social and technological power than of different value systems; worker-cultivator norms imply higher class behavior."

mind it would not be reasonable or natural for them to do otherwise.

In general the peasant is correct in imputing his motivations to the gentry. But he errs in attributing to them an energy and an ability to act in concert, which they do not possess. For example, some peasants think that the school has not been improved because the gentry intend to keep them illiterate in order to exploit them more readily. This argument assumes, of course, that the gentlemen are foresighted enough to make provision now for a situation which will exist 20 or 30 years hence, and that they have talked the matter over and have agreed upon a policy. In fact, the upper class, however selfish it may be in its attitude toward the peasant, is not capable of such effective action in this or any other matter.

An even more fantastic allegation—but one which is interesting for this very reason as an example of how far the peasant thinks the gentry will go in pursuit of their opposed *interesse* —is that the town officials deliberately suppressed a supply of circulars which told how to emigrate to America. If any such circulars existed, the reason they were not distributed was almost certainly ordinary indifference and incompetence. That, however, was not Pasquale's view of the matter:

They hid the circulars so that no one could go. They are afraid that if a worker goes to America he will get rich there and come back as a tourist and be in a better position than they are. They wouldn't be the top dogs any more. Also, they are afraid that if too many families leave there will be nothing left for them to do . . . no one left to work—and if no one works, how will they eat? For it's the peasant who does the work.

In the upper class view, the peasant has a specific character which is to be explained by *his* class position. He is stubborn, suspicious, secretive, and crafty. He never tells the truth. Dr. Gino describes with pained amusement the behavior of peasants who have known him all their lives and have always been well treated by him. They come to him with the greatest suspicion—as if by coming they were serving his purposes, not theirs —and lie about their symptoms. Women, the doctor says, are especially apt to conceal their ailments from him. When he asks where it hurts they say, "Here." But they wince when they are touched somewhere else. "It hurts here?" he will ask. "No," they will say. And so finally he has to guess.

They are so suspicious that if I were to visit them professionally and give them something, they would begin to wonder just how much the government is paying me that I can afford to come to their houses and give things away.

As the gentry sees it, the peasant's suspiciousness is a hang-over from centuries of oppression. There was a time (presumably now past) when he had to be suspicious to survive; suspiciousness, accordingly, has become deeply ingrained in his character—in fact, instinctive. Now he will not tell the truth under any circumstances.[12]

This, of course, is mostly myth. The peasant's secretiveness is by no means "instinctive"; he is willing to talk freely of his affairs when it is to his advantage to do so.[13]

To both sides, then, the gentry and the peasants, the war of all against all appears as a class war. Intellectuals who study the southern Italian society, influenced as all intellectuals must be by Marx, are prone to the same error.

12. Dr. Gino tells a story about a peasant father who throws his hat upon the ground. "What did I do?" he asks one of his sons. "You threw your hat upon the ground," the son answers, whereupon the father strikes him. He picks up his hat and asks another son, "What did I do?" "You picked up your hat," the son replies and gets a blow in his turn. "What did I do?" the father asks the third son. "I don't know," the smart one replies. "Remember, sons," the father concludes, "if someone asks you how many goats your father has, the answer is, you don't know."

13. The investigators had no difficulty getting answers from peasants. Upper class people were more reserved. From the standpoint of the peasant there was nothing to be feared from giving information to "the Americans"; they came from, and would soon return to, a different world. Moreover, many small favors and some large ones were to be had by cooperating. For the upper class, however, the situation was entirely different. For them, America was not so far away; who could tell how their information might be used? And for the upper class, who could not accept small loans and handouts of food and old clothes, there was no material incentive to cooperate.

7

Ethos in Principle

How men *do* behave and how they *should* behave are different matters. In the Montegrano view, a man is under the necessity of contending against brutal and capricious nature for the survival of his family. He must, therefore, be preoccupied with the *interesse* of the family and ready to do those things— including those ungenerous and unjust things—which will serve its advantage. Knowing that all other men are under the same necessity, he must fear their aggression and protect himself against it by remaining aloof or by striking first when that can be done safely.

Montegrano's conception of how men should behave has of course been influenced by the Catholic Church. It would be a mistake, however, to suppose that the Montegrano view is even approximately that of the church.

The Montegranesi get little religious instruction. A peasant grandmother tells her grandchildren the stories of miracles and sacred things which she heard from her grandmother. At six a child learns his catechism, a meagre list of questions and answers which is likely to be forgotten soon after the priest has given a simple test. In school an hour a week is devoted to religion. In later life the individual, if he goes to church—and many do not—hears simple sermons: the priest says, for example, that to be a good Catholic one must love God, obey the laws of the church, and do right. On saints' days speakers sometimes come from Naples and Potenza to tell about the saint whose holiday it is.

This is the extent of the ordinary person's religious training. Those few who could read the Bible are not discouraged from doing so but they are not encouraged either. A few peasant women have prayer books or the gospels, but most homes contain no religious literature.

Every peasant has his children baptized but (according to a Montegrano priest) most of them—especially the men—do not take seriously the idea of life after death. They believe there may be some kind of an after-world but that, whatever its nature, it will be the same for all. The hope of heaven and the fear of hell do not move them.

For the typical peasant, God (or Christ, the terms are used interchangeably) is not a spirit of loving kindness or even of firm justice. He is a demanding and capricious overlord. He may not notice one at all. If He does, He may distribute bounty or catastrophe according to whim.

Many think of God as a hostile, aggressive force which must be propitiated. A young woman, very angry with her father for getting drunk and making it necessary for her to leave a *festa* to take him home, sobbed, "What do I have to do to satisfy Christ? He never does any nice things for me, and He always does these bad things to me. I don't know what to do to satisfy Him."

Some Montegranesi pray more to the saints than to God. Candles are rarely left before the main altar; most people think it more economical to leave them before the statue of a saint or madonna.[1]

1. The most popular saint is S. Antonio di Padova, who in Montegrano (but not elsewhere!) is the protector of animals and thus of the peasant himself. S. Pasquale is the protector of women; those who are concerned about making a good marriage—and therefore plain girls especially—bring candles to him. S. Giovanni Battista is the protector of the town; he is worshipped on public occasions. S. Rocco, the protector against plagues, is the most popular saint in nearby Basso, a fetid town in the valley; his vogue may have spread to Montegrano from there.

Five Madonnas are honored in Montegrano, and for some people the

These judgments are made on practical grounds: no one has heard of any noteworthy miracles performed recently by God; this or that saint, on the other hand, has shown himself to be able and willing to afford protection (it is always protection that is asked) in a special class of matters. Some peasants even believe that certain saints are more powerful than God.

The differences among the saints, or between the saints and God, are believed to be more in power and accessibility than in character. Like God, the saints are capricious and demanding: however devotedly one serves them, one cannot be sure of their favor.

The relation between the believer and God (saint or madonna) is characteristically based on the *interesse* of each. One party wants to be honored with candles and masses. The other wants protection. If he has a dream which he interprets as a warning or if he is in a situation which is particularly risky— if his pig is sick, for example—the peasant may think it wise to buy help from one who can perform miracles. He is careful, of course, not to pay until the miracle has been performed; presumably he thinks that if the Deity were paid in advance He would not perform His part of the bargain since He could not be penalized. "If my pig does not die before I sell him," the peasant says, "then I will give S. Antonio two candles."

The priests are of course distressed at the peasants' impiety, but there is little they can do about it. If a priest reproaches him for placing candles before a saint instead of worshipping

---

connection between them and the mother of Christ is extremely vague. (When a Montegrano boy who had studied for the priesthood attempted to explain to an old woman that there is only one Madonna, she laughed at him. "You studied with the priests for eight years," she said, "and you haven't even learned the differences between the Madonnas!") The Madonnas are: (1) the Madonna of Pompei, whose miracles are well known in Montegrano; (2) the Madonna of Carmine, whose feast is celebrated in a nearby town; (3) the Madonna of Peace, who is honored in Montegrano with a feast and with a statue erected after World War I and to whom mothers prayed for their sons at war; (4) the Madonna of Assunta, the protectress of one of the Montegrano churches; and (5) the Madonna Addolorata, most commonly identified with the mother of Christ.

God, the peasant pays no attention; he thinks that the priest is acting on a mere whim or that he has made some private deal with God by which, for favors received, he undertakes to get Him candles at the expense of the saints.

¶   ¶   ¶

The ideas of right and wrong which are the peasant's own (which are not, that is, imposed upon him from the outside and imperfectly assimilated by him) relate mostly to the central theme of his existence: the family of procreation. Goodness and badness exist for him mainly in connection with two statuses, that of "parent" and that of "outsider-who-may-affect-the-family."[2]

In relation to the first of these statuses, goodness consists in working and sacrificing for the sake of the family, in giving the children the counsel they need to set them on the right road, and in being faithful to one's mate. (Faithfulness is of absolute importance in women; it is not equally important in men, but it is not unimportant either.)

In relation to the other status, that of outsider-who-may-affect-the-family, goodness consists in not having to be feared. The good man does not seduce another's wife or daughters, does not steal, and is not a troublemaker. The good woman is not covetous of her neighbors' possessions and does not gossip. Stated positively, the good person is amiable, minds his business, and does a favor for one in need.

2. One who is not viewed as a parent or as an outsider-who-may-affect-the-family is not judged at all. A group of peasants were asked what sentences they would give to each of the following: a thief, an assassin, a swindler, a rapist, one who seduces a wife or husband, an exploiter, and a prostitute. Savage sentences were given to all except the prostitute. About half the respondents would not punish her at all. "She is of no interest," some said. "It is her destiny," others said. The only one to give the prostitute a severe sentence was a woman who remarked, "These people ruin the family." The comments of the others showed that they felt the prostitute was the only one who did *not* represent a threat to the family.

The following definitions of the good man or woman (the first four by men and the others by women) are representative of peasant opinion:

Whoever goes stirring up people and doesn't leave them alone or is always trying to cheat—and this may be a man or a woman—is bad. Even in a discussion one can see quickly who is good and who is bad by their comportment when they speak. He also is bad who seeing someone cross his land begins to yell and reprove them even when there is no injury. A woman is good if she is honest [faithful] and minds her own business.

↑ ↑ ↑

He is a good man who has never done harm to anyone, treats everyone with good will, and unites with friends and others. He is bad, instead, who is haughty and is always looking out for his own affairs. A woman is bad who is mean to her husband and, above all, has a long tongue.

↑ ↑ ↑

He is a good man who is worthy. That is, he is not haughty and he is good with other people. A bad man is one who is discourteous and who does not know how to be a friend to anyone. A woman is good when she thinks of the affairs of her household, her husband, and her children. She is bad when she is a bad woman [unfaithful] or does not interest herself in her own affairs.

↑ ↑ ↑

He is a good man who interests himself in his family and thinks about the upbringing of his children and, further, who does some good for other people poorer than himself who have need. A woman is a good woman when she thinks about the welfare of her family and bad when she betrays her husband or seeks to instigate other bad things.

↑ ↑ ↑

A good man is one who is well disposed [has a *buon animo*], who has good feelings and thoughts toward others, is a good worker—is in fact all those things we think of as good. A bad man is a man with an ugly temper—a delinquent, unpleasant. In fact, when you say someone is bad you can mean many things—all the things we think of as bad. A good woman is a woman who is a good worker and virtuous. A "bad woman" can mean she is bad in many senses. She may be a woman of the streets—a lost woman as we say here— or she may be a malicious woman.

✝ ✝ ✝

A good man is a man who does not speak evil of other people, does not say harsh things to people, gives good advice, and does not dishonor his family by going with other women. A man who has a mistress is a bad man; he betrays his family and disgraces his children. A man who steals or carries tales is a bad man. A woman is good who respects the honor of her family, her husband, and her home by being faithful to her husband. An unmarried girl who is loose is a bad woman.

✝ ✝ ✝

A man or woman is good who demonstrates good will and is courteous toward others, is charitable when someone asks for something but, especially, minds his own business and doesn't criticize anyone or gossip. On the other hand, it is a bad man or woman who breaks the eggs in someone else's basket.

✝ ✝ ✝

A bad man is one who doesn't work, who goes to a wine cellar every night, beats his wife, and steals. A good woman is one who works hard, respects her husband, her family, and those around her. A bad woman is one who is lazy and dirty and who is always mixing herself up in other people's affairs.

In an effort to discover the relative importance of certain values (as well as the amount of consensus in the ordering of them) some peasants were asked to express preferences between alternatives of the following kind:

Which is better:

1. (a) she is anxious for her children to go to school and to raise themselves and therefore she sometimes beats them, (b) she is gentle

and kind with her children and content to let them remain what they are.

2. (a) he is a miser who works hard, (b) he is generous but a loafer.

3. (a) he tries hard to improve his children's position but he is proud, (b) he is not proud but he is content to let his children remain as they are.

4. (a) he married an ugly woman in order to get money for his sisters' dowries, (b) he married for love and let his sisters stay single.

5. (a) he provides poorly for his family but he is religious, (b) he is not religious but he provides well for his family.

Where—as in all of these choices—qualities which would serve the advantage of the family had to be weighed against qualities which, although valuable, would not serve it, there was a decided majority in favor of the family-serving qualities. The answers to the questions above were as follows:

Question	Number Respondents	Prefer (a)	Prefer (b)	Can't Decide
1	28	28	0	0
2	28	26	2	0
3	25	23	2	0
4	28	18	9	1
5	27	8	17	2

On the other hand, when qualities which might offer a threat to the family were weighed against others which, although disliked, did not offer a threat to it, the preference was heavily in favor of the non-threatening qualities. For example,

Which is better:

6. (a) she is amiable but she covets her neighbor's possessions, (b) she is often mean but she is not envious.

7. (a) she is avaricious but she never gossips, (b) she gossips but she is generous.

8. (a) she gossips but she is never cruel, (b) she is sometimes cruel but she never gossips.

9. (a) he is avaricious but he is a loyal friend, (b) he is generous but not especially loyal.

10. (a) he is pleasant and amiable but not steadfast, (b) he is a steadfast friend but often irritable and unpleasant.

11. (a) he is proud but he does not covet his neighbor's possessions, (b) he covets his neighbor's possessions but he is not proud.

12. (a) he is honest but he curses the saints and the priests, (b) he loves God but he is sometimes tricky.

The answers to these questions were as follows:

Question	Number Respondents	Prefer (a)	Prefer (b)	Can't Decide
6	28	5	23	0
7	25	20	4	1
8	25	8	15	2
9	25	23	2	0
10	25	7	18	0
11	25	16	9	0
12	28	19	8	1

Some questions posed a choice between alternatives in which family-serving qualities were coupled with family-threatening ones. Here, as one might expect, there was no consensus. Some people took one horn of the dilemma and some the other. For example:

Which is better:

13. (a) he protects the honor of his sisters carefully, but he tries to seduce other people's sisters, (b) he does not try to seduce girls and he is not very much concerned about his sisters' honor.

14. (a) he steals but he does not commit adultery, (b) he commits adultery but he does not steal.

15. (a) she is a gossip but she works hard, (b) she is lazy but she never gossips.

16. (a) he steals now and then but he is not lazy, (b) he never steals but he doesn't like work.

17. (a) he neglects his father and mother but he does not steal, (b) he takes good care of his father and mother but he steals often.

18. (a) he is anxious to advance his children's position but he is envious of his neighbors, (b) he is not envious but he is content to let his children remain what they are.

Here the answers were as follows:

Question	Number Respondents	Prefer (a)	Prefer (b)	Can't Decide
13	28	14	12	2
14	28	11	15	2
15	28	16	11	1
16	28	16	12	0
17	28	14	11	3
18	28	16	9	3

In comments accompanying their answers many made it clear that they judged all questions by the single criterion of advantage or threat to the family. No matter what the question or the answer, the answer was likely to be justified by: "It is better for the family," or "it harms no one."[3]

𝟏 𝟏 𝟏

In the Montegrano view, action is the result more of forces playing upon the individual than of motivations arising within him. The individual is indeed naturally impulsive; his impulses incline him toward bodily pleasures and in general toward self-indulgence. Unless checked by other forces, they lead him—from heedlessness rather than malice—to do wrong. Usually, however, impulses are checked and action is redirected by external forces.

3. Whether a certain quality was regarded as family-serving or family-threatening depended in some cases on how the respondent identified. Respondents making different identifications would give opposite answers although employing the same criterion. Thus, for example, in question 18 above, some of those who preferred (b) did so because they identified with the envier rather than with the one envied, e.g., "I would prefer without a doubt to be envious and to be able to change the position of my children." Even among those who identified with the envier, different answers were possible, for some thought envy might be self-defeating: e.g., "I prefer (b) because it is generally said, 'He who envies bursts,' and thus if an individual is envious of his neighbors it will be difficult to advance his children and thus it is better to leave them alone and not to envy anyone." The questionnaire would have been better had the questions necessitated a predictable identification, e.g., which is better, a *father* who . . . or a *neighbor* who . . .

The most potent check is the fear of bodily injury. In Montegrano physical punishment is used freely to inculcate a proper spirit. Children and even young men and women—especially girls who are willful in the choice of a husband—are struck or beaten. In an unusual case, a girl in her twenties who insisted upon a marriage which her mother opposed was deprived of a dowry, refused food, and severely clubbed.[4]

Another check is "advice." In the Montegrano view, one who suppresses an impulse to do wrong does so because he remembers the advice of his parents: he remembers, for example, their having told him that one who steals is likely to go to jail. The advice of parents would be acted upon more often if it were not for companions. They invariably tempt one to follow impulse. They do this by giving advice also, but "bad advice." Thus in a characteristic TAT story:

> There was a young man who always disobeyed his parents and never listened to their advice. Every day he became worse and worse and followed bad company—friends who led him always even farther down bad paths. He began to steal and commit bad actions; but one day he was caught with some friends while stealing and was taken to prison. But with his cleverness he was able to escape from prison and he remained many days hidden in the woods. Then he was caught and condemned to prison and so for not having listened to the advice of his parents he found himself badly off and had to end his days in prison. (14)

This assmumption that conduct is largely formed by the influences that play upon one helps to explain, perhaps, why the southern Italian takes such extraordinary precautions to

---

4. In such cases a daughter is not altogether without power, as the following TAT story illustrates: "A girl of 15 years fell in love with a young man and loved him very much, but her parents were not willing. She did not know what to do. She finally decided to commit a bad action that might in the end force her parents to give their permission. And thus it happened. When her parents knew that the girl was to have a child, they gave their permission and sought to hurry the marriage. Afterwards everyone was very happy. (7)

protect the chastity of his women. A foreigner, seeing how elaborately the women are guarded, is likely at first to suppose that the southerners are a remarkably lusty people and to suspect that, despite the precautions, their hot-bloodedness must express itself in a high rate of illegitimacy and in much adultery and related crimes of passion. He finds on inquiry, however, that the illegitimacy rate is not extremely high (five per 100), that adultery is rare, and that crimes of passion are very few. Objectively there seems to be little reason for concern over the honor of the ladies. Yet the southerners are obsessed with the subject. Why? Perhaps because in the general view the woman who is not forced to be chaste ceases to be so. The situation must be managed so that she has no opportunity, or, if that is impossible, so that she will fear the consequences. In the Montegrano TAT stories, a husband or father who discovers his wife or daughter with a lover "kills them both without giving the matter a moment's thought."

This view of behavior as externally caused has the characteristics of a self-fulfilling prophecy, of course. In a society in which everyone believes that a man and woman will make love if they are not restrained from doing so by outward circumstances, a man who finds himself alone with a woman is virtually compelled to make love, for not to do so would imply a question about her charms or his virility. And a woman in such circumstances, knowing that women who are tempted often forget the advice of their parents, is likely to forget the advice of hers. In other matters the principle is the same.

In the Montegrano view, one who does evil ought to be punished with the greatest severity, for blame and punishment contribute to the pressure without which everyone would be led into evil. One who suffers punishment does not, however, feel guilty. Instead he feels unfortunate. Like Pinocchio, he may reproach himself for not having listened to the advice of his parents, but he knows that the evil lies outside himself: it was his misfortune to have listened to the wrong advisers. He was stupid in this, perhaps, but not evil. It is they—the advisers

—who are evil, not he. It was bad luck that he should have come under pressure from them rather than from others.[5]

It is not too much to say that most people of Montegrano have no morality except, perhaps, that which requires service to the family.[6] If a peasant resists an impulse to do wrong, it is because he fears the law or public opinion, not because he is led to do right by love of God, conscience, or the fear of punishment after death. In fact, "good" and "bad" are seldom used in a moral sense at all. To "do wrong" usually means to "act so as to bring punishment or misfortune upon oneself." To say that one action is "better" than another means only that it is more expedient. A peasant says that one who curses the saints is better than one who steals "because God pardons; if one steals, one may have to face the law and the law does not pardon." Another explains that an adulterer is better than a thief because "if he gets caught the adulterer gets a beating, while the other ends in jail." To the peasant, the "better" man is the one who performs the "better" action, and the "better" action is the one which is most advantageous.

The difference between moral and other valuation is that the former employs standards which are felt to be obligatory. Standards are obligatory when they are in some way associated with what is sacred. Because they are sacred, their violation is

5. When Pinocchio learns that he is becoming a donkey he cries, "Oh poor me! Poor me!" "My dear one," replies the Marmot, "what can you do? Now it is destiny. It is written in the decrees of wisdom that all boys who are lazy and who dislike books, schools, and teachers . . . are transformed into so many little donkeys." "But the blame is not mine," Pinocchio says. "The blame, believe it, little Marmot, is all Candlewick's . . . I want to return home: I want to be obedient . . . but Candlewick said to me, 'Why do you bother yourself with studying . . . ?'" "And why did you follow the advice of that false friend, of that bad companion?" "Why? Because I am a puppet without judgment . . ."

6. Even this does not always operate. Until a generation ago, infants, including ones born in wedlock, were not uncommonly abandoned in Montegrano. Moreover, when emigration was at its height, fathers who went to the New World often failed to send for their wives and children. The vast amount of talk about the duty of the parent to the family, equal to the talk about the duty of female chastity, may signify a sense of insecurity on this point too.

felt as guilt. For most of the people of Montegrano, nothing is sacred. This being so, they feel neither obligation nor guilt. As a Montegrano priest put it,

The major part of our people do not even consider the possibility of evaluating their acts; for these people morality is what most people do or it is what is legal, for they do not believe in the spiritual life or in punishment after death.

The implications of all this for political life are clear. The state exists to force men to be good. A regime is worthy of respect if it has plenty of power and uses it rigorously to enforce obedience and to maintain law and order. A regime which uses its power solely to enforce the law and not to exploit the citizen comes into being only when the rich and powerful take it into their heads to indulge themselves in the virtues of charity and justice. This does not occur very often, and there is nothing the citizen can do to bring it about; like other good things, good government is obtained by luck, not achieved by effort, enterprise, and sacrifice.

*   *   *

One might expect that in a society so preoccupied with *interesse* and so untrammelled by a sense of obligation to kin, neighborhood, or community, the war of all against all would break out in violence. In fact Montegrano is reasonably law-abiding. In 1954 there were no murders, abductions, or acts of carnal violence. There were 24 cases of theft and 15 of assault and assault and battery. Two persons were arrested for drunkenness and two for slander, and there were 29 cases of trespassing and seven of wrongful pasturing.[7]

Two features of the situation sharply limit the possibilities

7. In some of these cases the offenders were probably people who came from other towns to the fair. It is possible, too, of course, that some Montegrano people got in trouble elsewhere.

In the judicial district of which Montegrano is a part and which comprises eight towns with a total population of 20,000, there were the following arrests during 1954: murder, none; abduction, none; carnal violence, none; theft, 131; assault and battery, 124; drunkenness, 17; slander, 32; trespass, 191; and wrong pasturing, 58.

for gain by violent, illegal, or unfair means. One is that the criminal law is sternly enforced. A pair of *carabinieri* with carbines over their shoulders is always within hailing distance, and a man may get six months in jail for cutting down a tree which does not belong to him. The other is that there is danger of reprisals from people who feel themselves injured. In a village so small and isolated there is no way to elude enemies for very long. There was a time when an injured party could work his revenge in secret by the use of magic. Nowadays it is not quite so serious to have an enemy; few people take the witches or the "evil eye" seriously.[8] But an enemy can still

8. There used to be witches in Montegrano who could ruin whole families, but they are all dead now, Prato says. Other people, including two or three old hags who take presents for casting or undoing spells, disagree with this judgment and say that there are spells of four degrees of seriousness: (1) "tied" (*legato*)—this type is like a knot and is easily undone; (2) "underground" (*sottoterra*)—this is more difficult, but digging (metaphorically speaking) will uncover the evil; (3) "drowned" (*annegato*)—still more difficult, but it is possible in principle to find the body, i.e., the source of the evil; and (4) "burned" (*bruciato*)—here the case is hopeless because when a thing has been consumed by fire nothing can be found.

If Dr. Gino's prescriptions do not help them, believers in witchcraft assume that their illness belongs to the magical rather than to the medical realm and go to the witch for treatment. The usual first assumption, however, is that a complaint is medical.

On these matters John McDonald has commented in a personal communication, "Witches and the evil-eye have been losing their importance in Calabria, too. They are usually only used after the failure of more 'rational' methods or complementary to them."

Even those who scoff at witches are apt to pay heed to certain common superstitions. From the standpoint of this chapter, one of the most interesting superstitions is the belief that invidious comment, even though made to flatter, will bring harm to the one who is put in the enviable light. Thus a mother told a group of ladies that when she was nursing her second child she had so much milk that she had to wear a rubber guard to avoid soiling her clothes. One day when she was visiting a friend the milk began flowing and continued until there was a puddle on the floor. Her friend remarked, "How lucky you are. And here am I, who cannot produce a drop." On her return home the woman found that her breasts were dry. They remained dry, and she was unable to nurse her next babies.

find hidden ways to do harm. Prato had an enemy who stole into his fields at night and cut down his young fruit trees. This was an injury against which there was no possible protection. Gossip is another danger against which one cannot protect oneself. If, for example, his enemy spreads a rumor about Maria, Prato would be undone. Under such circumstances, one takes pains to avoid making enemies. They, too, are a luxury.

Vanity, or the desire to be liked or admired, is also a curb on aggression, but its importance is by no means as great as the others. One would be ashamed (i.e., embarrassed) to be caught stealing, for example, but the risk of being ashamed is a light thing in comparison to that of going to jail or being beaten. One likes to be considered a fine fellow. ("My wife gives food to people who need it when we have it to spare because the next day you feel good when you see the person you helped pass by and you know he is saying to himself, 'Now there's a man who helped me.' ") But the satisfaction of being thought well of would not, for most people, outweigh any advantage that could be had without danger by trickery or other unfair means. In short, the desire for the good opinion of others is a supporting but not a leading motive.[9]

9. Some remote settlements in the mountains above Montegrano are virtually cut off from the larger society. Teachers, doctors, and priests never penetrate to them. The *carabinieri* visit them only when murders are reported. Among these mountaineers social life apparently comes very close to being a war of all against all. When mountain people come to town for a fair, the townspeople treat them in the most gingerly fashion; "they would as soon stick you with a knife as talk with you," the townspeople say. This is not merely an expression of the normal tendency to traduce the people of other places; the mountaineers really are rough. But even among the mountaineers, there are some restraints on aggression: magic still has a powerful hold on them (and so the physically strong must fear the weak), and kinship obligations seem to be stronger and more far-reaching than in Montegrano.

8

Origins of the Ethos

THE mechanism which produces the ethos of amoral familism is undoubtedly complex, consisting of many elements in a mutually reinforcing relation. The dreadful poverty of the region and the degraded status of those who do manual labor, matters which were discussed at length in Chapters Three and Four, are surely of very great importance in forming it; they are structural features, so to speak, in the system of causes. If we turn now to other elements in the system, it is not to depreciate the importance of these.

One of these other elements—and one which itself seems to be of structural importance—is the fear of premature death which is so pervasive in Montegrano. As an earlier chapter showed, the Montegranesi are extraordinarily apprehensive. They are fearful, especially, that they may take sick and die, leaving their children "on the street," or that the children themselves may die. Fifteen of the sixteen Montegranesi tested told TAT stories about the unexpected natural death of a parent or child. Altogether they told 45 such stories. That this preoccupation is unusual may be seen from the fact that only two of the 10 northern Italian peasants tested told such stories (these told one each) and only 12 of the 30 Kansans told them (these told 16).

One of the TAT pictures shows a boy contemplating a violin which lies on a table before him. Eleven of the 16

Montegranesi saw the boy as an orphan; of these, eight saw him as a beggar, one as dying of hunger, one as mistreated by a miserly uncle, and one as a neglected bastard. The boy was not an orphan or a beggar for any of the northern Italians; most of them thought he was an ambitious lad highly motivated to become a violinist. Of the 30 Kansans, none thought he was an orphan or a beggar (although five called him "poor"); 13 said he was being forced against his will to practice.[1]

That fear of premature death and of leaving one's children "on the street" should so preoccupy the people of Montegrano is not surprising. Until after the Second World War, when anti-biotics came into common use, the death rate there was high—never less than 15 per 1,000 and in some years probably as much as 40 or 50. Until recently the probability that a child would lose one or both of its parents before coming to maturity was high.

Not only was the death rate high. Poverty was (and is) so acute that most parents could make no provision for the support of their children in the event of their deaths. To be an orphan almost always meant to be a beggar as well.

Many of the people who are now so fearful lest their children become orphans were orphans themselves. Others were brought up by step-fathers or step-mothers. Until a few years ago it was a fortunate child who lived out his childhood with both natural parents.

Even when both parents lived, children were (and are) often sent at a very early age to earn their keep among strangers as servants and apprentices. The cruel *padrone* is as familiar to the Montegrano imagination as the cruel step-parent and step-sibling.

The importance of such childhood experiences is unmistakable in many life histories. Prato, for example, can hardly remember his father, who died when he was a small child. His mother remarried and, according to him, treated the children of her second husband much better than those of her first. At the age of 11 or 12, he was sent out as a servant. His later child-

1. The stories told about this picture are reproduced in Appendix B.

hood memories are of unrelieved misery—of looking after live-stock in the winter rain, of going for wood in deep snow, of being hungry. His step-sister, with whom he was later on bad terms, bossed him with a stick.

His wife remembers that when she was a very small child her step-mother would send her and her sisters from the room while she fed milk and eggs to her own children. She and her sisters got only bread and not always enough of that. At six she went into domestic service in Calabria. Every morning, she carried water from a fountain to a house. "I would rather have my children die than live the kind of a life I lived," she said.

Maria Vitello's mother and father died at the ages of 33 and 36, leaving five children. She was sent to relatives in Naples as a servant. Of her childhood she said,

I remember most being maltreated and hungry. I was often beaten. I beat my children today but it is a light thing in compari-son. I remember something that used to happen over and over again. My aunt would send me to the store to buy three-quarters of a *kilo* of *rachitelli* [a kind of macaroni]. All the way to the store I would say to myself, "*rachitelli, rachitelli.*" Then when I got to the store somehow it would come out "*vermicelli*" [a different kind of maca-roni]. When dinner came everyone would have his dish of macaroni except me. My plate would be empty. I would go hungry. Some-times my uncle would get drunk and beat me.

Pasqualina's father died a few days before she was born. Her mother remarried and had three more children. The step-father was kind, but before long he went off to America. In time he wrote to his wife to join him and sent her money. She sold their house and land, bought clothes in which to travel, and made ready to sail. Eight days before the scheduled de-parture the father cabled that they were not to come. His employer, he said, would not keep him if his family were there. After that he never wrote again, and the mother supported five children as best she could. Her disappointment left her "nerv-ous." "I don't think anyone—even in those days—got more beatings than I did," Pasqualina recalls.

✓ ✓ ✓

Of course, people elsewhere have had much the same experience. Throughout most of history and in most parts of the world, parents could expect to die young. Not everywhere, however, has this made people as apprehensive as they are in Montegrano. Obviously other circumstances must be taken into account to explain the Montegrano ethos.

Family organization is one such circumstance. In some societies the family is large enough and strong enough to offer assurance that the death of the parents will not mean catastrophe for the children. Where the extended family exists, a child whose parent dies is still part of the family. In some cases the child even feels as strong an attachment to uncles and aunts as to mother and father. In other cases (e.g., the Russian *mir* of the last century) the main attachment is to the community as a whole. In such societies the loss of parents may be of little importance; there are plenty of others to take their place. If the attachment of the child to the extended family or community is strong, that to its natural parents may be correspondingly weak. In this case the emotional shock of the parent's death is less.

With a few exceptions, (see Table 11) Montegrano households consist of the members of one nuclear family and of no others besides. Not living with grandfathers and grandmothers and uncles and aunts and not regarding them as members of the family in a real sense, the Montegrano child—unlike the one who is brought up in an extended family—sees his parents as his only possible source of protection, support, and affection. He supposes that if they die he will be "on the street." In Montegrano an orphan does not move into the household of relatives as a matter of course. They may not be able or willing to take him at all. If they are, he may have to work as a servant; at best he cannot expect to be treated as an equal by them. Montegrano has many Cinderellas.

The hypothesis that the extraordinary apprehensiveness of the Montegranesi was produced by two factors in association —a high death rate *and* the absence of the extended family— could be disproved by showing that the same apprehensiveness exists also among a people who have the extended family (though it could not be proved correct by the *lack* of such an example). It happens that in the province of Rovigo in northern Italy such families have existed for several generations. They were described by a nineteenth century traveller as follows:

> I remember, when I was a boy half a century ago, I used, in the autumn holidays, to make excursions to the neighborhood of Padua where I was acquainted with some families of authentic peasants . . . The families were not small units, composed of a husband, a wife and a child or two, but great patriarchal groups, aggregations of several families, connected by ties of blood, who collectively worked a farm of which they were tenants. Usually it was let to the whole race of them, and they obeyed the orders of their chief, who was the oldest man among them, the father, grandfather, greatgrandfather of the various generations represented in the community. What nestfuls of children! Hardly did I appear in the yard before they emerged from all sides, running to meet me in their tens because they knew I could teach them new games and scatter some half-pence among them. There was only one kitchen, and the girls and the Titianesque brides were responsible in turns for the cooking . . .[2]

Some of these families are to be found today. Thematic Apperception Tests of 10 peasants who grew up in "stem" families in the province of Rovigo revealed a striking absence of the fearfulness so characteristic of the Montegranesi. As Tables 3 and 4 in Chapter Six and the first pages of the present chapter have shown, the northern peasant is not preoccupied with the prospect of calamity and sudden death.[3]

Whether or not "stem" families have relieved anxiety about the possible death of parents in Rovigo, they seem to have trained the peasant to act organizationally. In these families the

2. Quoted by Helen Douglas Irvine in *The Making of Rural Europe*, George Allen and Unwin Ltd., London, 1923, p. 37.

3. Of course family type is not the only important difference between the northern and the southern peasant. The northerners tested had more education, were in closer touch with the modern world, and were relativly well off.

father (or, if he is dead, the eldest brother) organizes the labor force of the family and superintends all its affairs. There was a time when he was an autocrat. Nowadays he takes advice from a council of his sons and sons-in-law. Subject to his authority and that of the council, each of them has responsibility for one part of the joint enterprise: one son looks after the animals, another does the marketing, and so on. Profits are shared according to work done and disputes are arbitrated by the head of the family.

Either because they have learned in the family to subject themselves to the discipline of a group or for other reasons, the peasants of Rovigo, unlike those of Montegrano, are able to work together. Some participate in a farmers' association and there are cheese-making and other cooperative undertakings in the district.

✔ ✔ ✔

If we ask why the peasants of Montegrano did not develop the institution of the extended family, the answer is perhaps to be found principally in the circumstances of land tenure. Patriarchal or "stem" families could exist only where peasants could get reasonably secure possession of adequate amounts of land. In the Po Valley and center of Italy, the feudal system ended and land became an alienable commodity long before the Unification.[4] Many of the wealthy retained their lands and took an active part in the development of a progressive agriculture. These wealthy owners found it to their advantage to rent land to large families of peasants on a more or less permanent basis. Having relative security on a sizeable tract, the peasant family had an incentive not only to increase its numbers so that it would not have to employ labor but also to accept the discipline of a single head who would plan and direct the work of all. Even today "stem" families are the most numerous among renters who produce tobacco, rice, hemp, and other labor-intensive crops.

4. The historical contrast drawn here is based on McDonald, *op. cit.*

In much of the south, on the other hand, feudalism survived almost undisturbed until the Napoleonic Wars. Land was the inalienable property of the aristocracy of church and state. During the nineteenth century feudalism was gradually abrogated. Feudal desmesnes were made marketable and many cultivators of the south bought them. After Unification, high taxes forced many petty owners who had gone in debt for land to sell it to the few who had capital. In some places the nobility continued to hold large estates; unlike the large owners of the north, however, these were absentees who took no interest in the management of their property. Petty proprietors bought them out in some places; these generally worked the land with hired hands rather than through renters. The peasants accordingly had neither incentive nor opportunity to organize a family to provide labor and management for the enterprise. Meanwhile population increased rapidly and small farms became smaller by inheritance. For more than a generation there have been few farms in Montegrano large enough to support more than a small, nuclear family. As Table 11, Appendix A, shows, there are only 27 "stem" families in Montegrano; all but four of these live on farms.

✓ ✓ ✓

What has been said so far may help to explain the apprehensiveness of the Montegranesi, but it does not explain other aspects of their ethos, especially their selfishness in all relations except that of parents to children, and their tendency to think of the individual as moved principally by forces outside of himself.

Some light on these matters may be gained from an account —albeit a sketchy one—of childhood training in Montegrano.

The arrival of a child is always celebrated as a joyous event, but in those homes where there are already three or four children the new one, after its first reception, is likely to be regarded with mixed feelings, especially by the older sisters who will have to be responsible for much of its care.

Peasant babies are swaddled immediately after birth and kept swaddled until they are from five to seven months old. Twenty years ago the baby's arms were tied down by the swaddling; nowadays they remain free. A peasant mother fastens her swaddled baby in a basket and carries it to the fields where it dangles from a tree while she works. Some upper class women swaddle their children briefly or not at all.

Babies are usually nursed for about a year, but if they reach that age at the beginning of summer, the nursing may be continued because of the difficulty in hot weather of finding food which will not cause enteritis and diarrhea. A few women nurse for longer periods in an effort to prevent conception, but this is uncommon.[5]

It is taken for granted that it is useless to try to toilet train a child before it has reached the age of two. If a young child makes a mess on the floor, the parents may point out to it where it should go, but they do not become annoyed or angry. Usually children have "trained themselves" by the time they are two-and-a-half or three.

Before she is four a girl is told to keep her dress down. Boys are not taught modesty so soon.

Even those children who are not wanted get a great deal of petting and affectionate play from parents and older siblings. In general, the parents are extremely permissive.

Children are punished when they are naughty, however, and sometimes even when they are not. Parents and teachers believe that an occasional blow helps a child grow up to be more "refined" and to "find itself better off in life." As a mother explained,

> It can be said with justice according to the proverb, "Slaps and spanks make nice children"—and the mother spanks because she wishes them well.

5. There are great variations in these practices from one town to another, a circumstance which should afford opportunities to test theories regarding the effects of specific practices on personality development. For example, in a town near Montegrano, the women do not carry their babies to the fields; instead they wean them as soon as possible and leave them in others' care.

As a rule, the parent exercises influence over his children by punishing or threatening to punish rather than by offering rewards or appealing either to the child's desire to please or (in the case of older children) to its willingness to cooperate on grounds of mutual respect. A TAT story by a 17-year-old girl is interesting because of what it reveals about the normal and abnormal in these matters:

There was a terrible little girl who was very naughty and continually angered her mother. Many times her mother beat her hoping to make her more calm but nothing happened. One day the mother promised her a pretty doll if she would only be good. The little girl did become good and when the mother bought her a doll the little girl kept it with her always, night and day, and she was no longer naughty. Now she is grown and married and has two children of her own. (7)

Sometimes the anger smoldering inside a peasant breaks out suddenly and vents itself upon the children. Many adults in Montegrano remember dreadful beatings which they received now and then from one parent or the other. Such outbursts are comparatively rare nowadays. Whether that is so or not, most people seem to think that an occasional outburst is of no great importance if the parent is affectionate in between times. Of 28 peasants who were asked which is better, a man who loves his children but beats them when he is drunk or a man who never pays much attention to them, 21 said the first, six said the second, and one was unable to decide.

To improve their characters, or perhaps merely for entertainment, children may be frightened with horror stories about death and other gruesome subjects. How memorable these experiences may be is suggested by a TAT story told by a young man:

This picture represents the figures of death as they used to describe it when we were children in order to frighten us, and apropos of this . . . this is what happened to a friend of mine. One night they were talking about death and how ugly death is and that sometimes death appeared to a person in order to take that person away forever. Then the boy went away with a great fear of death. In fact, that night he dreamed that death had appeared to him to take him away with her. Such was his fright that he fainted and was ill for two days. (15)

That children will be impudent, willful, selfish, ungrateful, and full of naughty tricks is taken for granted. Naughty tricks will be punished with blows, of course, and in the end the child will thank its parents for having made so many sacrifices for it and having set it upon the right road.

In his autobiography Paolo Vitello tells with great relish of the many Pinocchio-like tricks he played as a child—how at the age of five he nearly set his little sister on fire when he lit a straw cigarette while his parents were away, how he teased his uncle into killing a lamb which belonged to his father and then hid the carcass under the bed, how when his father sent him to the store to buy nails he bought a pipe instead, how he gathered poisonous weeds for the rabbits instead of grass, and so on. After all these tricks Vitello was beaten, but it is clear from his account that both he and his parents regarded his naughtiness not only as cute but also as evidence of a lively and enterprising spirit.

It is relevant here to note that such childish naughtiness consists typically of deception. The child practices being "foxy" (*furbo*) by deceiving his parents. They enter into the game by punishing him (for if there were no risk there could be no game!), but they also stand on the sidelines, so to speak, and applaud his cleverness.

Any illness is treated with great concern in Montegrano, and a child who suffers from an indisposition is pampered. Most parents consider that their children are "delicate." When Vitello had measles he was kept out of school a whole year. In this there was nothing unusual.

Punishment, although freely given, does not entail any suggestion of withdrawal of love by the parent, and it often has no connection with a principle of right and wrong. In his autobiography, Prato tells how when he was a small boy he became the favorite of a young priest who came from Naples to visit in Montegrano:

One day [Prato says] I went to the public square and some honest men who were there told me that if I would make ten somersaults they would give me some money. I made them promptly, and they gave me 40 centimes. I brought the money to my mother who was surprised, but I explained it to her. She told it to the priest who was very angry because the somersaults could be very dangerous to me. He bound my hands behind my back and gave me only a slice of bread and a glass of water for 24 hours.

In this story the priest exhibits a characteristic hypersensitivity to the question of health, a characteristic severity in punishment, and a characteristic failure to establish a relationship between the punishment and an antecedent wrong-doing. Prato was not punished because he had done wrong to somersault; he was punished to teach him that doing somersaults would be dangerous. (Whether his account of the incident is accurate or not is of no consequence here, of course; this at least is what he now supposes to be intelligible behavior.

An older boy's naughtiness is carried on with "bad companions." Vitello's autobiography continues:

Paolo already had become worse and disobedient. In fact, he had a close friendship with two other boys who taught him even more bad habits. Paolo, although a big boy now, was still timid and these friends, by taking him along with them, destroyed the timidity. They taught him to dance and to play the mandolin and together they would go about playing serenades.

Pranks and punishments followed one after another. One prank was a love affair.

And so Paolo began to make love and one time he was surprised by the parent of a girl while he and the girl were in a shack together. But he escaped marrying the girl.

At sixteen he was still a naughty boy and, in retrospect, he is proud of his naughtiness. The autobiography continues:

He was sixteen when one night his father forbade him to leave the house because of a failing on his part. But instead some friends let him know that there was to be dancing at F— that night, so Paolo found the means to escape from home. At the dance they all got drunk and as they walked home they dropped their instruments on the ground. When Paolo returned to his home, he found his father waiting up for him. The usual blows followed. We see that Paolo, notwithstanding all the blows rained upon him, kept always his own character.

In the Montegrano view a child's natural indolence and naughtiness are overcome only by the strenuous exertions of its parents. They must force the child to take the right road. The typical parent-child relation is that of Geppetto to Pinocchio: the father long-suffering and forgiving, the child cruelly exploiting his love until finally overcome with remorse. The Pinocchio story is repeated again and again in one form or another. Here, for example, is a TAT story told by Vitello:

Two parents had an only son and they were willing to undergo all kinds of sacrifices in order to see that their son learned a profession better than theirs. But the son did not appreciate their sacrifices. In fact, he would not study and liked instead to go and play and make bad companions. His parents tried in every way. They punished him many times but it did no good because he was very willful. Many times they would close him in his room but instead of studying he would go to sleep. Years passed and the boy grew up. Then he wished to make reparations, but then it was too late. His parents had grown quite old and thus he had to go to work in order to live. He was very, very sorry that he wasn't able to do anything but hoe the ground. (1)

Not surprisingly, a grown-up Pinocchio thinks of himself as still a child who ought to gratify his mother by making her will his. The following TAT story was told by Vitello about a picture showing an elderly woman standing with her back turned toward a tall young man:

A poor woman, a widow, had made so many sacrifices to raise her only son, but this young man at 18 fell in love with a girl who, first of all, was not suitable. And besides, the mother wanted him to finish his studies first, while he wished to abandon them in order to marry. Because his mother absolutely did not want it, he one day escaped from the house and went far away. The mother, poor thing, remained desolate and did not know what to do. But her son,

who was really a good child, after a while understood that he had
done something bad when he left his mother because it had been she
who had raised him, and now he had left her alone. After a few
days he returned to the house and threw himself at the feet of his
mother, crying and begging her pardon. She, out of her great joy,
pardoned him. From then on they lived happily. (6 BM)

When Pinocchio does finally marry it is hard for him to stop
being a wayward boy. He would like to run away from his
wife as he did from his mother, and he would like also to come
crawling home like a good boy to beg forgiveness. Here is
another TAT story by Vitello:

There was a man who had a wife and many children but he was
corrupt with bad habits and did not wish to work. He squandered
all his money by gambling and was causing his family to die of
hunger. Until finally it ended with his fighting with his wife and he
left the house in search of a fortune. But after a while he began to
be sorry. He thought constantly of his children and of his wife, left
in misery, and so one fine day he gathered his courage and returned
home. From then on by his work the family was able to live. (15)

In this account of childhood in Montegrano, two things
stand out as of special importance:

1. The indulgence of parents toward children and their
willingness to allow children to be selfish and irresponsible—
"carefree"--until all at once at the time of marriage the grown
child must assume the burden of looking after a family of its
own.[6] Perhaps it is not too much to say that the Montegranesi
act like selfish children because they are brought up as selfish
children.

2. The reliance upon blows to direct behavior and the capricious manner in which punishment is given. Punishment, it

6. Peasant parents are indulgent toward children of both sexes, but
girls are not permitted to be carefree. A girl begins very early to keep
house and to take care of younger children. When she is about 16 she
begins work on her *corredo*, the sewing and embroidery of which keep
her busy for years. Propriety requires that she be confined to the house
under the eye of her parents and older brothers. Resistance to parental
authority—but not naughtiness—is more or less expected of her.

has been noted, is unrelated to any principle of "oughtness"; at one moment the parent kisses and at the next he cuffs. If gratification and deprivation—"good" and "bad"—depend upon the caprice of one who has power, no general principles can be internalized as conscience. The individual may try to propitiate the power holder, but he will not be surprised if his efforts fail and he receives ill when he deserves good. To receive ill will be "bad fortune" and to receive good will be "good fortune." Neither, of course, will have any relation to principle. Having no internalized principles to guide him, the individual will depend upon the promise of rewards and punishments to tell him how to act. The punishment he receives will serve the function of the guilt he would feel if he had a conscience. His relation to all holders of power—the state and God, for example —will be formed on the model supplied by his parents.

9

The Future

THAT the Montegranesi are prisoners of their family-centered ethos—that because of it they cannot act concertedly or in the common good—is a fundamental impediment to their economic and other progress. There are other impediments of pervasive importance, of course, especially poverty, ignorance, and a status system which leaves the peasant almost outside the larger society. It would be foolish to say that one element in this system is *the* cause of backwardness: all these elements—and no doubt many others as well—are in a reciprocal relation; each is both a cause and an effect of all of the others. The view taken here is that for purposes of analysis and policy the moral basis of the society may usefully be regarded as the strategic, or limiting, factor. That is to say, the situation may be understood, or altered, better from this standpoint than from any other.[1]

Amoral familism is not a normal state of culture. It could not exist for long if there were not an outside agency—the state—to maintain order and in other respects to mitigate its effects. Except for the intervention of the state, the war of all against all would sooner or later erupt into open violence, and

1. See the discussion of the concept of the strategic (or limiting) factor in Chester I. Barnard, *The Functions of the Executive*, Harvard University Press, 1938, pp. 202–205.

the local society would either perish or produce cultural forms —perhaps a religion of great authority—which would be the functional equivalent of the "social contract" philosophers used to write about.[2] Because the larger society has prevented indigenous adaptation of this kind without making possible the full assimilation to itself of the local culture, the Montegrano ethos exists as something transitional, and in this sense, unnatural.

Clearly a change in ethos cannot be brought about by the deliberate choice of the people of Montegrano. It is precisely their inability to act concertedly in the public interest which is the problem. And besides, how can a people "choose" a morality? If they could choose it, it would be because they already possessed it.

The possibility of planned change depends upon the presence of an "outside" group with the desire and ability to bring it about. If all Italians were amoral familists, no such group would exist. In fact, the political left, the church, and the industry of the north all contain elements which might inspire and support reform in the south.[3]

2. It is tempting to compare the ethos of the Montegranesi with that of their very early ancestors as described by Fustel de Coulanges in *The Ancient City*. The early Indo-Europeans were amoral familists too, but their families consisted of thousands of persons and the bonds within the family were immensely strong.

3. It must be acknowledged that there is danger of the spread of amoral familism from the south. J. S. McDonald has written in a personal communication:

"There is some evidence that the Montegrano ethos may be spreading in Italy. The proportion of southerners in Rome's large immigrant population has been rising progressively. They probably will not alter the main structure of Rome's formal organization, just as the Montegrano folk have not destroyed what the state has given them. However, such a lot of southerners at the top of Italy's administrative hierarchy and social elite may have depressing repercussions. On the other hand, my work in Australia suggests that Veneti do have a welcome effect on Calabresi: in two towns here I have found Veneti leading Calabresi into formal and informal economic and recreational organizations. Southern Italians are, I feel, much less critical of northerners than vice versa; in

Nevertheless, it may be impossible to bring about the changes that are needed. There is no evidence that the ethos of a people can be changed according to plan. It is one thing to engineer consent by the techniques of mass manipulation; to change a people's fundamental view of the world is quite a different thing, perhaps especially if the change is in the direction of a more complicated and demanding morality.

It must be acknowledged, too, that the Montegrano economy would not develop dramatically even if the villagers cooperated like bees; establishing an ambulance service, for example, might make the village a more nearly tolerable place in which to live, but it would not contribute materially to its economic development. Although it would be foolish to deny that a talented entrepreneur might use organization to accomplish the seemingly impossible, the sad fact is that Montegrano's isolation and relative lack of resources give it a comparative disadvantage which no amount of cooperation can overcome. Some small irrigation facilities might be established by group enterprise, and these might make possible a small cannery; at best, however, such developments would have little impact on the poverty of the village. Nevertheless, the ability to act concertedly might, if it was marked, eventually have important economic effects, albeit ones visible far from the village itself. Group action to improve the schools, for example, might have the effect in the long run of enabling the young Montegranesi to enter a larger labor market and to enter it on more favorable terms. Group action might also eventually increase trans-oceanic migration, thus relieving the pressure of population on local resources. In comparison with these indirect effects, the direct ones immediately visible in the village would probably be negligible.

In order for concerted action—and therefore economic development either in the village or elsewhere—to take place, it

---

fact, they admire them in many ways. This attitude bodes well for the assimilation of southern to northern Italy if close communication can be established and the northerners are not amoralized in the process."

would not, of course, be necessary that amoral familism be replaced by altruism. Indeed, individualism (or familism) is a very good thing from an economic standpoint, provided it is not so extreme as to render concerted action altogether impossible. In some underdeveloped lands, economic development can take place only when bonds of custom and tradition which prevent the individual from acting rationally in his self-interest are loosened or broken. Such societies present more difficult problems to the planner than does one in which people can be depended upon—as the Montegranesi can—to act on the basis of rational calculation. The villagers' anxiety to get ahead and their readiness to adapt themselves, morally and otherwise, to whatever is conducive to their material well-being must be counted great advantages from this standpoint.

However, amoral familism must be modified in at least three respects in order for organization, and thus economic and political progress, to be possible:

1. The individual must define self or family interest less narrowly than material, short-run advantage. He need not cease to be family-minded or even selfish, but—some of the time, at least—he must pursue a "larger" self-interest. For example, he might prefer to take some of his income in prestige or in the intrinsic satisfaction of organizational behavior as a "game" rather than in material reward. Or he might forego present for future advantage, for example by establishing a reputation for fair dealing. At the minimum no more than what is usually called "enlightened" self-interest would be necessary. "I do not think, on the whole, that there is more selfishness among us than in America," Tocqueville remarked, "the only difference is that there it is enlightened, here it is not. Each American knows when to sacrifice some of his private interests to save the rest; we want to save everything, and often we lose it all."[4]

2. A few persons, at least, must have the moral capacity to act as leaders. These need not act altruistically either; they may lead because they are paid to do so. But whether they give

4. *Democracy in America*, Knopf edition, Vol. II, p. 123.

leadership or sell it, they must be able to act responsibly in organizational roles and to create and inspire morale in organization.[5]

3. Voters and others must not destroy organization gratuitously or out of spite or envy; that is, they must be willing to tolerate it when it does not interfere with them.

In attempting to create these minimal conditions, two general approaches are open to planners. One is to eliminate the underlying conditions which produce the objectionable features of the ethos of amoral familism and to create instead conditions which will "naturally"—i.e., without further interference by the planners—produce an ethos consistent with the essential requirements of economic and political development. This approach depends crucially upon the possibility of identifying and changing the key elements in the causal system, something which may be impossible.

One of the difficulties in the way of manipulating the causal elements is change. Certainly the complex of causes which produced the ethos of amoral familism is changing rapidly and in fundamental respects. According to the view taken here, high death rate and the related fear of orphanage and neglect were of decisive importance in forming the Montegrano ethos. Today, however, because of antibiotics, the death rate is very low. Whereas a few years ago it was a rare child who grew up with both natural parents, now it is a rare one who does not. The drop in the death rate has been accompanied by a less dramatic drop in the birth rate. Most young peasant couples are trying to have two children and no more. To the extent that they succeed, the personality and ethos of the new generation will doubtless be changed. To grow up as one of two children in a family including the natural parents is an altogether different experience than to grow up as an orphan or as one of several half-brothers and half-sisters.

The dreadful poverty of the Montegranesi also helped to form their ethos. Poverty is no less today, nor is it likely to be

5. See the discussion of the moral functions of the executive by Barnard, *op. cit.*, especially Ch. XVII.

in the foreseeable future. Indeed, by an objective measure—for example, per capita consumption of protein—most villagers are probably somewhat worse off than were their grandparents, the productivity of whose land had not been reduced by erosion and depletion. At any rate, whatever may be the actual trend of their consumption, the Montegranesi *feel* it to be less, for their wants are vastly greater now than before; what was satisfying to their fathers and grandfathers is intensely dissatisfying to them.

This is especially true in the matter of status, and, as it was argued above, *la misèria* is as much or more the result of humiliation as of hunger, fatigue, and anxiety. The contempt of the upper class for the peasant may be somewhat less now than it was a generation ago. About this it is very difficult to judge. But it is clear that in the last twenty years the peasant has become far more sensitive to his inferiority, and it seems likely that his sensitivity will grow fast, while the others' contempt diminishes slowly.[6]

Such changes will not at once be reflected in a new ethos. The present ethos will tend to perpetuate itself for a long time, even though many of the circumstances which gave rise to it no longer exist or no longer operate in the old way. Long established ways of thinking and valuing have a life of their own independent of the particular conditions which gave rise to them. This is what has been called "cultural lag."

It will be seen, therefore, that it is not sufficient for the planner to change the situation which produced the present ethos. He must estimate the nature and rate of development of the ethos which will emerge when the new conditions finally make themselves fully felt. Of course, this must be mostly a matter of guesswork.

6. Wartime studies showed that American soldiers were most dissatisfied with their rank in those units where opportunity for promotion was greatest. The writer has the impression that the same phenomenon may be observed among American Negroes. As his opportunities for mobility improve, the peasant may become more hostile and aggressive as well as less miserable.

Some guesses may be made with confidence, however. If the average income were increased by a large amount, people would sooner or later act on a broader conception of self-interest.[7] In other words, the rate at which prestige, the intrinsic satisfaction of work, and other such non-material rewards would be substituted for material ones would increase with income. There would be an accompanying increase in the number and importance of public service roles, i.e., roles which people are paid (in money or other satisfactions) to assume. If communications between the south and the rest of Italy—and indeed the rest of the world—were greatly improved, the standards of other places would rapidly gain acceptance in the villages. If free movement of labor between occupations and between regions were permitted and encouraged the standards and habits of the south would be quickly changed. If manual labor were to lose its stigma and the peasant were to have a dignified status and opportunity for social mobility, a new spirit would soon be evident.

Obviously, however, these changes are not likely to occur. How, despite the much improved economic situation of Italy as a whole, is the income of the south to be greatly increased? How, short of wholesale migration—an event which the north would regard as a catastrophe—is the southern peasant to acquire the ways of the north? And how, as long as he is miserably poor, is the peasant's degradation to be relieved?

Changing the ethos, if it could be done deliberately, would entail some dangers. Eliminating the conditions which gave the present ethos its peculiar character would not assure that the new ethos would not have other features that would be worse. It would be too bad if the planner succeeded in changing indifferent Fascists into ardent Nazis. Moreover, there is the danger that the objectionable features of the ethos may serve latent functions of the greatest importance. The concept of

7. The village of southern France described by Wylie, *op. cit.*, exemplifies, perhaps, the adaptation the ethos of amoral familism would make to improved economic circumstances. The average income in Peyrane seems to be at least twice that in Montegrano.

interesse, for example, may have a latent symbolic function which transcends its manifest one. To devalue the concept *interesse* may be to devalue the family as well.

The other general approach open to the planner is the manipulation, not of the underlying situation, but of the actors themselves. For all practical purposes, this is the "old-fashioned" technique of education. Probably the best education for the people of Montegrano would be to have among them for two or three decades a couple of dozen middle and upper class families who felt a sense of civic responsibility and who would serve in a more or less self-conscious way as teachers and leaders. This is not feasible, however. Even if persons with the required qualities existed in sufficient numbers and even if they were willing to live in poor, backward, isolated places like Montegrano, it would be impossible to afford them suitable occupational roles in such places.

The change in outlook that is needed might conceivably come as the by-product of Protestant missionary activity.[8] There is little prospect, however, that Protestants will be permitted to proselytize in southern Italy.

A more nearly practicable possibility (it would be better to say, a less obviously impracticable one!) might be to carry on educational efforts from provincial centers through a special staff of government workers assigned to cultivate a sense of community responsibility. The extreme centralization of power in the hands of the prefect, which is now one of the conditions preventing the development of a competent political style in the villages, could be used to further an educational program. Instead of approving or disapproving local measures

8. In Brazil Protestantism is reported to have created among its adherents an unprecedented participation in group affairs and to have reduced illiteracy, dishonesty, and gambling. See Emilio Willems, "Protestantism as a Factor of Culture Change in Brazil," *Economic Development and Cultural Change*, Vol. III, No. 4, July 1955, pp. 321–333.

If the Roman Catholic Church assigned priests from northern Europe and the United States to missionary work in southern Italy, very much the same effect might be produced. But this apparently is out of the question also.

on purely bureaucratic grounds as at present, the prefects might make progress toward responsible local action in the public interest a condition of approval. At present it would be futile for a delegation from Montegrano to go to the prefect with a plan for, say, an ambulance service. The prefect would have no authority in the matter or, if he had, he would be unwilling to share it. This is one reason why Montegrano people do not make such proposals. If, however, the prefect's office were administered with educational objectives in mind, he might tell the officials and leading citizens of several towns that if they could agree upon a workable plan he would approve it and help them put it into effect. In short, the centralized power now used to frustrate local action could be used to promote it. Proposals to reduce the power of the prefect are unwise if the possibility exists of changing the character of the office.

The suggestion made here is for the rapid devolution of as many governmental functions as possible from the ministries in Rome first to the provincial prefects and then from them to local bodies which demonstrate capacity for self-government. The function of the prefects in this process would be essentially two-fold: (a) to encourage local action and to reward it with resources and authority, and (b) to prevent corruption—and eventually the cynical assumption that corruption exists—by maintaining the closest watch on the manner in which public functions are performed.

Improvement of the schools should be the first concern of such an administration. The minimum schooling guaranteed by the constitution should in fact be provided everywhere and it should be made clear that gifted children of any social class will be sent out of the village to continue their schooling at public expense. Extraordinary efforts should be made to bring devoted teachers into the villages; a rotation plan which would give them incentives to serve in remote villages and guarantee them an eventual return to the city might help. At any rate, teachers should be made to feel that they are part of a national network and that there is no danger of their getting "lost" intellectually or professionally in a village. Vocational training should be widely offered, but in the skills needed in industry rather than agriculture. (Unless the peasantry is pushed off the land to make farms larger, a commercial agriculture employing modern techniques is impossible in most of the south.

Measures to improve the schools would have the interest and support of the villagers. Formal education has always been an avenue—indeed the *only* avenue—of social mobility. To have it opened to him would give the peasant the sense he lacks of being a valued member of the larger society. The individualistic character of the ethos would, of course, assist, not impede, the spread of education: when education is a practicable way of getting ahead of one's neighbors, it is eagerly sought.

Public television might be used to advantage in adult education, as it has been in Puerto Rico, but in the long run establishment of independent weekly newspapers serving districts of two or three villages would probably be more valuable. A local newspaper would give the peasants an incentive to learn to read (why should one learn to read if he lives where there is nothing to read?), but it would do much more besides. It would create a sense of community, a conception of a common good, and an agenda for public-spirited action.

If the administration of local affairs were fully decentralized, this in itself might bring an independent local press spontaneously into existence. When local public opinion has power to decide issues of importance, there exists an incentive for someone to attempt to mold that opinion. "The more numerous local powers are," Tocqueville observed, ". . . the more profusely do newspapers abound."[9]

Teachers and other local leaders should assist the villagers to undertake simple ventures in cooperation and community action. Perhaps the best starting place would be the organization of village soccer teams. Although few villagers have ever seen the game properly played, they have a great deal of interest in it. (When the returns of important games come over the radio, even peasants gather at the bar to hear them.

9. *Op. cit.,* p. 112.

Recently some Montegrano boys formed teams. They had to quit after one game, however, because Mayor Spomo refused them the use of the only suitable field.) A soccer team would give a few people experience in cooperation without overtaxing their ability to cooperate. It would also help to draw the upper and lower classes together: in southern states, as in America, a good athlete is admired regardless of his social status, and there is no doubt that upper and lower class boys would play together as equals in Montegrano. Having a team in common would give the gentry and the peasants something to talk to each other about. It would help to create a sense of community. Games between villages would give rise to a "we" feeling and when a district winner went off to play in national competition, some identification would doubtless be felt with the district and even with the nation.

Success in one such venture might lead to others of more tangible value—to the formation of a credit union, perhaps, or of business enterprises organized for profit.

The upper class should be encouraged to take leadership in local affairs. Italian observers are apt to conclude that the southern gentry are so full of hate for each other and for the lower classes that nothing constructive can be expected of them. The example of Montegrano suggests that this is an exaggeration, or at least that there are exceptions to the rule. There it is not class antagonism which makes the gentry indifferent to the common good; rather it is the same concept of *interesse* which affects the whole society, and the gentry, although self-interested, are less narrowly so than the others. Because of their better education, moreover, they are more open to reasonable discussion and persuasion. It is even possible that books like this one may find readers in the upper class and that some of them may be influenced to take a slightly different view of the local society and of their place in it.

*   *   *

Unfortunately it is necessary to end this discussion on a cheerless note. If all of the measures that have been suggested here were pursued actively and effectively, there would be no dramatic improvement in the economic position of the village. These measures would lighten somewhat the heavy burden of humiliation which the peasant bears and this might dissipate the grim melancholia—*la misèria*—which has been the fixed mood of the village for longer than anyone can remember. But even with humiliation gone, hunger, fatigue, and anxiety would remain. Under the best of circumstances, it will be a very long time before the people of Montegrano have enough to eat.

Nor would there be a dramatic change in the ethos of the Montegranesi if such measures as these were carried out. Under the most favorable conditions it might take two or three or four generations for nature to restore and reinvigorate the social bonds which have been withered and desiccated for a century or more.

Finally, it must be said that there is little likelihood that any such measures will be tried. Even if it were certain—which it is not, of course—that they would work, they probably would not be tried. Nations do not remake themselves in fundamental ways by deliberate intention any more than do villages.

Appendix A

Education and Illiteracy, Land Use, Levels of Living, Age at Death

Table 1—Amount of Education (highest grade completed), Persons 21 Years of Age and Over, Montegrano, 1954

	LESS THAN ELEMENTARY		ELEMENTARY SCHOOL (5 GRADES)		MIDDLE SCHOOL (6– 8 GRADES)		UNIVERSITY (OVER 8 GRADES)		ALL	
	No.	%	No.	%	No.	%	No.	%	No.	%
Males	299	32.7	568	62.1	21	2.3	27	2.9	915	100
Females	681	62.4	393	36.0	3	.3	14	1.3	1091	100
All	980	48.9	961	47.9	24	1.2	41	2.0	2006	100

Source: Municipal records.

Table 2—Illiteracy by Class, Persons Aged 10–39, Montegrano, 1951

Class*	Percent Illiterate
Laborer	30
Farmer (country-dweller)	44
Farmer (town-dweller)	18
Artisan	8
Merchant	9
Office Worker	12
Professional	10
Landed Proprietor	19
All	29

* A person belongs to a given class if the head of the household in which he lives belongs to that class. The illiterates in the office worker and professional categories are women.

It is doubtful how much significance can be attached to these data. Apparently all those who have finished five grades of school are *ipso facto* counted as literate; in fact, many who have been out of school a few years can read or write only a few words. It seems certain that by any reasonable standard the number of illiterates would be higher than that shown here.

Source: Census schedules.

Table 3—Land Use in Montegrano, 1954

Use	Acres	Percent
All	17,433	100
Unproductive	2,028	12
Forest	3,280	19
Pasture	4,834	27
Orchards	916	5
Cultivated	5,735	33
Fallow	640	4

Source: Local tax records.

Table 4—Use of Cultivated Land in Montegrano, 1954

Use	Acres		Percent
All	5,732		100
Vegetables	170		3
Dry beans		74	
Irrigated Vegetables		96	
Cultivated trees and specialties	598		10
Olives		129	
Grapes		363	
Figs		106	
Grain	2,815		50
Wheat		2,519	
Barley and Oats		247	
Corn		49	
Forage	2,149		37

Source: Local tax records.

Table 5—Numbers of Farms by Size of Farm, and Percentage of All Cultivated Land in Farms of Various Sizes, Montegrano, 1951

Size of Farm (acres)	Number of Farms	Total Area (acres)	Percentage of All Cultivated Land
Under 2.5	114	148	2.6
2.5–7	235	1257	22.1
7.5–14	108	980	17.3
15–24	56	1111	19.5
25–50	23	942	16.6
Over 50	14	1247	21.9
All farms	550	5685	100.0
All commercial farms (50 acres and over)	93	3300	58.0

Source: Local tax records.

Table 6—Income of a Montegrano Farm Laborer Family, Year Ending October 31, 1955

	Days Employed	Cash Wage	EARNINGS IN KIND		Total Earnings	Net Value Farm Products[1]	Gifts[2]
			Meals	Other			
Father	180	$114.30	$ 62.33	$28.06	$204.69	$	$
Mother	38	8.87	14.11	2.42	25.40		
Daughter	116	42.66	28.06	.48	71.20		
Son	51	10.61	20.24	.32	31.17		
All	385	176.44	124.74	31.28	332.46	107.25	14.51

Total Income [3]—$482.22

1. Includes 9 bushels of wheat worth $29, vegetables worth $10, and home produced meat worth $90 minus $21.75 for cash farm expenses. No deduction value has been attributed to labor.

2. Includes $12.09 given to the girl by her grandmother for her trousseau.

3. During the year the family received an additional $12.09 which had been earned previously and $38.25 for various services to a visiting social scientist. This last sum is not listed above because it was not normal income, i.e., it would not have been earned except for the accident of the visitor's presence.

Table 7—Expenses of a Montegrano Farm Laborer Family, Year Ending October 31, 1955

FOOD

Grain (641 lbs.)	$37.63	
Macaroni and spaghetti (153 lbs.)	16.85	
Flour (61 lbs.)	4.51	
Salt (87 lbs.)	3.20	
Wine (3 gallons)	3.16	
Potatoes (272 lbs.)	2.00	
Meat (5.5 lbs.)	2.00	
Olive Oil (2 qts.)	1.29	
Sugar (2.6 lbs.)	.59	
Fish (1.5 lbs.)	.45	
Vinegar	.35	
Onions	.16	
Milling of grain	.89	$ 73.08

CLOTHING

Shoes (purchase and maintenance)	18.91	
Bed linens	9.70	
Trousseau	74.41	
Other	15.79	118.81

HOUSEHOLD

Soap	4.51	
Fuel	.98	
Alarm clock	4.83	
Barber	.69	
Paint	1.45	
Miscellaneous	5.20	17.66

DEBT REPAYMENT

		10.48

MEDICAL

		.08

FARM

Lamb	5.32	
Taxes	3.76	
Fertilizer	.32	
Rent of harrow	1.60	
Blacksmith	3.00	
Basket	1.28	
Pick axe	.96	
Chicken wire	.96	
Miscellaneous	4.55	21.75

GRAND TOTAL $241.86

Table 8—Minimum Corredo (Trousseau) for a Farm Laborer's Daughter

12 sheets	$ 38.69
24 pillow cases	11.28
12 nightgowns	9.67
8 slips	9.02
8 table cloths and napkins for six	25.79
4 table cloths and napkins for twelve	58.03
1 light blanket	12.90
1 wool blanket	22.56
3 coverlets	14.51
1 blanket (puff)	8.06
pots and pans	24.18
1 linen chest	8.06
1 grain chest	16.12
4 mattresses	32.24
1 straw mattress	8.06
12 towels	9.07
4 grain sacks	3.22
tableware	4.83
baskets	4.83
12 pairs of stockings	5.80
3 pairs of shoes	11.00
5 dresses	24.18
	$362.10

Table 9—Percentage Distribution of Age at Death, All Deaths, 1948–53, Peasants and Others, Montegrano

Age at Death	Peasants—%	Others—%
1 year or less	20.8	8.1
13 months–7 years	6.2	—
8–30	4.2	8.1
31–60	15.6	14.3
61–80	37.6	28.6
over 80	15.6	40.9
All	100.0	100.0

Source: Municipal records.

Table 10—Expenses of an Artisan Family, Year Ending December 1, 1955

FOOD

Grain (110 lbs.)	$ 6.40	
Milling of grain	3.00	
Macaroni and spaghetti (212 lbs.)	22.08	
Salt (40 lbs.)	1.16	
Wine (6.5 qts.)	1.68	
Meat (17.5 lbs.)	6.37	
Fish (29.7 lbs.)	8.71	
Cheese (5 lbs.)	3.80	
Olive Oil (1 litre)	.61	
Candy	2.12	
Fruit and vegetables	10.61	
Eggs (11 doz.)	4.00	
Sugar (8.5 lbs.)	1.87	
Other	2.40	$ 74.81

CLOTHING

Shoes (purchase and maintenance)	26.30	
Bed linens	6.09	
Umbrella	1.76	
Other	29.47	63.62

HOUSEHOLD

Soap	3.18	
Fuel and Electricity	12.03	
Barber	.61	
Home repairs	53.33	
Wedding gift	2.40	
Nursery school	2.90	
Miscellaneous	9.40	83.85

DEBT REPAYMENT 2.40

MEDICAL

Doctor	6.40	
Medicines	40.93	47.33

FARM

Threshing and grinding	3.47	
Pig	14.40	
Taxes	5.42	
Hired labor	8.12	
Fertilizer	16.16	
Pig feed	6.42	
Rent of oxen	1.92	
Miscellaneous	1.54	57.45

GRAND TOTAL $329.46

Table 11—Composition of Households by Social Class, Montegrano 1951

	LABORER No.	FARMER No.	ARTISAN—MERCHANT No.	UPPER CLASS No.	OTHER No.	ALL FAMILIES No.	%
Category I							
A. Nuclear Family (husband—wife—children)	128	192	63	27	21	431	
B. Incomplete Nuclear Family (widow or widower—children)	16	33	1	5	14	69	
C. Extended Family (husband—wife—children—one or more relatives)	13	29	7	11	7	67	
All	157	254	71	43	42	567	70.1
Category II							
A. Stem Family (husband—wife—unmarried children—married son and his family)	2	23	1	1	—	27	
B. Incomplete Stem Family (widow or widower—unmarried children—married son and his family)	—	3	—	—	3	6	
C. Fraternal Joint Family (married brothers and their families)	—	—	—	—	—	—	
D. Married Brothers and Sisters and their Families	—	—	—	—	—	—	
All	2	26	1	1	3	33	4.1
Category III							
A. Childless Couples	19	21	7	5	20	72	
B. Brothers and Sisters	2	1	—	3	1	7	
C. Unrelated Persons	2	—	—	—	—	2	
D. Miscellaneous Composition	26	21	7	16	58	128	
All	49	43	14	24	79	209	25.8
TOTAL	208	323	86	68	124	809	100.0

Note: The categories are taken from Donald S. Pitkin, "Land Tenure and Family Organization in an Italian Village," Ph.D. thesis, Harvard University, 1954, p. 111.

Appendix B

Responses to a Thematic Apperception Test

Here are reproduced the responses of all Italian and some representative Kansas subjects to one thematic apperception test picture, that of a boy contemplating a violin which lies on a table before him. The Italians were all agricultural laborers or petty proprietors; the northerners had more education and income than the southerners. All of the northerners and all of the adult southerners were married and had children. The rural Kansans were also married. For the Kansas TAT's the writer is indebted to Professor Bert Kaplan of the University of Kansas. The Kansas TAT's are not considered representative of a rural-American ethos; they are included here only to provide a contrast which will highlight what is characteristically Italian in the others.

SOUTHERN ITALIAN
(MONTEGRANO)

1. *Man, age 47.* There was a poor boy who was an orphan and had been left nothing by his parents. He had nothing to live on, but in order to live during the day he would play his guitar and thus earn something. One day, however, some urchins began to laugh at him and since he answered them back, these urchins broke his guitar, and so the poor boy found

himself desperate because he had lost everything that he had and nothing was left to him except the blackest despair. One of the boys, however, repented and felt sorry for what he had done and took the little boy to his home where he could work and earn.

2. *Woman, age 34.* There was a little boy who had been left an orphan and he was very sad and unhappy. He thought surely this must be the end for him. In fact he was not able to study or work because he was very little, and thus the future for him looked sad, and the only thing that remained was for him to go out and beg alms and that is what he did.

3. *Woman, age 41.* A little boy, left an orphan, lived by begging, charity, and by playing his guitar. One day his one possession, that is the guitar, broke and the child cried because he no longer knew what to do. Then a gentleman saw him and gave him a new guitar.

4. *Man, age 32.* Two parents had an only son and so they were willing to undergo all kinds of sacrifices in order to see that their son learned a profession better than theirs. But the son did not appreciate their sacrifices. In fact he would not study and liked instead to go play and gain bad companions. His parents tried in every way. They punished him many times, but it did no good because he was very lazy. Many times they would close him in his room, but instead of studying he would go to sleep. Years passed and the boy grew up. Then he became aware of the evil he had done and wished to make amends, but then it was too late. His parents had grown quite old, and thus he had to go to work in order to live. He was very, very sorry that he wasn't able to do anything but go hoe the ground.

5. *Man, age 30.* There was a poor boy who had been left as an orphan and he had nothing to live on but charity. One day someone gave him a guitar. It was a little old. The boy thought that if he could only succeed in learning to play it well he might very well make his fortune, and so from morning until

night he would try to learn something about it, never ceasing and never tiring. One day a gentleman saw him who was much moved with compassion by him. The gentleman took the boy home and let him study. The boy knew very well how to profit by his good fortune and indeed became a very fine maestro.

6. *Woman, age 37.* There was a boy who cried continuously because he couldn't succeed in learning to play, and he was constantly unhappy about it. But he continued with his intention and finally after many struggles and much effort he ended up well and succeeded in becoming a very good artist.

7. *Woman, age 29.* There was a poor boy whose father and mother had both died and he was left very poor. He wondered how he could get by, and finally he decided the only thing he could do would be to go around playing his guitar and begging alms. And in fact this was the way he spent his whole life.

8. *Man, age 40.* There was a boy who from the time he was little made little instruments out of paper, so much enamored was he of music. But he was not able to go to school because his family had not the means. However he was not discouraged and continued by himself to learn something. How many times he would cry because he wasn't able to make happen what he wanted to happen. But then finally he was able to become a member of a small orchestra, and from then on his ability became in a short while excellent. He became a fine player and a musician of great fame.

9. *Woman, age 30.* There was a young boy in a poor family who wanted very much to study, but there was no possibility. Even during intervals of work he always sought to learn something. Then finally it was his fortune that an uncle from America sent him money so that he could study and he became a fine professional.

10. *Woman, age 36.* There was a poor lad who had been left an orphan, both his mother and his father having died. And

having no one else, he was truly poor. He spent his day playing a guitar and begging for alms. When night came, he slept wherever he found himself. One night he was very tired, having played all day without having earned a thing. It was already night-time and he found himself, as it happened, near a railroad track. And without thinking that a train might come by, he sat down on the track. Then he became very sleepy and then came the tragedy. A train did come and the poor child was found all in bits.

11. *Man, age 58.* Here we have a picture of a boy in front of a guitar and he seems very sad. Perhaps it is because he has been left without parents and now he is thinking of what he can do to earn his bread. And he decides to go and play the guitar in the streets, begging alms until he finds work.

12. *Boy, age 18.* This boy has lost his mother, and now he is very sad because he doesn't know what to do at this moment because, being a bastard, he has no one. He is thinking sadly of the misery he must bear, but it will not be like that because the father who had ignored him will look after him, send him to school, and start him on a good path.

13. *Girl, age 18.* There is a poor child left without mother or father and dying of hunger. One day he was given a guitar and he decided to play it in the streets and thus he earned something which allowed him to live. In the end, when he had grown older he found work and could be more at peace. Then he married and now he is happy.

14. *Girl, age 17.* There was a family that lived happily and well until both parents died within a short time of each other, leaving a nine-year-old boy who was given to the care of an uncle who was supposed to look after his well-being. But the uncle, who was a miser, treated the boy very badly. The boy, alone and sad, cried continually without being noticed. And thus he had to live for a long time until, becoming older, he succeeded in freeing himself from the tutelage of his uncle. Thus he lived more happily.

15. *Boy, age 18.* Here is a sad little boy. He is the son of a well-to-do family. He had a particular affection and attachment for a little guitar which he preferred above all others of his toys. But one day while he was amusing himself playing the guitar it fell and broke. He cried hard, notwithstanding the promise of his parents that he would have a new one just like the old one. Certainly this would not have happened if we were dealing with the story of a peasant's child.

16. *Man, age 42.* This little boy has certainly had a lot of sorrows. First his mother died. Then his father died and he was left alone. In order to live he went about playing in the streets, but one day even the guitar, which one could say was the sole source of life to him, broke and became good for nothing. That is why the child is sad—because he is thinking that he was born to this earth only to bear sorrows and that he will never have any peace. But one day his fortune changed because a gentleman interested himself in the boy, took him off the street, and put him in a college to study, and then afterwards he got a good job.

NORTHERN ITALIAN
(ROVIGO)

1. *Man, age 37.* There was a boy whose parents were not rich, but had only just enough to get by on. From the time he was little he was weak in health and unwell, so that he was often near death. He had been sent to school for some time, but studies fatigued him, and the boy suffered because he could not be like the other children. He spent his time at home sitting by the radio listening to music, and this seemed to interest him very much. Whenever the band came to town, he never lost the opportunity to hear all the music, and many times his parents would hear him singing over at home music that he had heard. One day the boy heard a beggar playing a violin and he was impressed by what it was possible to do with that instrument. From then on, the boy thought of nothing else, and he decided that he would like to be able to play the

violin. For many days he said nothing about it to his parents. Perhaps he thought that they would not be able to satisfy him because the instrument was expensive. His parents, however, seeing him sad and more thoughtful than usual, asked him why he had changed so. The boy then told them what he intended to do. The parents made some sacrifices and bought the boy a violin because they wanted to make him happy. They even sent him to town to a music master. The boy wishes at all costs to succeed because he has a passion for music. He spends many hours a day practicing his violin so that when he is grown up he will be a fine violinist and will be able to repay his parents for their sacrifices and expenses on his behalf. In fact he will become a good violinist and he will make his parents, who did so much and sacrificed for him, very happy.

2. *Woman, age 28.* There was the son of a great musician, a violinist. The son loved the father very much, and when the father played, the son never missed the occasion of listening to him. One day the father, while playing in a theatre, felt very ill but he continued to play all the same. The boy, however, was aware of this, and as soon as the father finished playing his piece the son ran out to see his father who had been carried to a room, the father having fainted. He found him near the end of his life because of an unexpected paralysis. The father, when he saw his son, told him that he would die happy if he would promise him that he would learn to play the violin, and the boy said that he would without fail. The father dies, and the boy does not give himself any peace from the absence of his father. But he does not have the courage to pick the violin up in his hands even though he wants to study . . . because he hates the instrument which deprived him of his father. Finally he succeeds in overcoming his melancholy and he begins to study with passion first of all because he had promised his father, and then because of the great passion he has himself. Like his father he will be a great artist.

3. *Man, age 32.* Here is a little boy all wound up in his own thoughts. He is sitting in front of a little table on which there

is an illustrated newspaper spread out. The boy is looking at a weapon. It is a particular moment in the life of the world, and the little boy has learned what is happening in Hungary where a people is rebelling against slavery. He is looking at the weapon and he is wondering how he can make it function and how he can use it. They boy has always been happy-go-lucky, but now the stories of the things that have happened and photographs seen in the newspapers awaken his fantasy. He would like to help that suffering people, but he does not know what to do because he is little. But his inclination to want to help them is still there even though he does not know how to help. He feels rancor against those who have caused these things, and this feeling will follow him until he is a man. He will never be able to forget all of the things he has heard, and when he is grown his thoughts will always turn to that part of the world where there are so many people who suffer. He will continue to condemn and to hate all those who have behaved so inhumanely toward the Hungarian people.

4. *Woman, age 34.* A little girl is thoughtful because she finds herself far away from her family. She is thinking about her mother who is far away from her and whom she has not seen for a long time. The mother has left her alone, and the little girl is always thinking about her and wishing to see her as soon as it is possible. The mother of the little girl was a very capricious woman who loved her little girl but put her in a boarding school in order not to have her with her because she wished to be free, and the child hindered her by her presence from doing what she wanted. The father did not oppose the capriciousness of the mother, and now the little girl is in the boarding school. She does not like it there because she wanted to be at home with her mother, but her mother has abandoned her anyway, and she will remain in the boarding school for many years yet. When the child is grown she will certainly not be able to pardon her mother for having kept her far away and for having neglected her in favor of her capriciousness.

5. *Man, age 36.* This is a boy who is thinking about how he wants to play the guitar, but up to now he has not succeeded in doing what he wants and has not so far even succeeded in understanding how to do it. He has in front of him a book which is to teach one to play without a teacher, but after a while he was not able to play as the book said. He is thoughtful on this account, but he will study some more because he wishes to become a fine guitarist. He wants to study in order to better his condition and to be able to have, one day, a better life. The boy is very intelligent. His parents are peasants, but the boy has shown himself to be so interested in this study that they have sought to make him happy by letting him study his instrument in order that they might one day have the satisfaction of seeing him achieve what he wishes. The boy will succeed in becoming a fine guitarist because his thought is fixed on this. He will leave his parents when he has learned his instrument well, and he will go and play in a dance orchestra, and he will make a good position for himself. His parents will be very happy about him and his job, remembering the hard work they had to bear in order to go forward in life.

6. *Woman, age 41.* This boy is seated in front of a table where there is a violin and some sheets of music. He is very thoughtful because he does not succeed in learning to play the violin, but everything is difficult at the beginning. His music teacher gave him some music to learn to play, but the boy tried it for a long time, and now he is discouraged because he has not succeeded in playing it as he wished. He is tired and he has put the instrument down and now he is looking at it. The boy, however, is willing, and if at the beginning it does not turn out very well, in time he will learn and he will become a great artist. The parents allowed him to study because they had not yet thought about what he could be when he grew up. When the boy said that he wished to learn to play the violin, his parents did not oppose him because they wanted their son to be what he liked.

7. *Man, age 50.* A boy was left at home to study. His parents had left him alone at home because they had to go out, and they told him to be good and to study and to do his school lessons. But the boy, after his parents had gone, soon got tired of studying and began to wander about the house looking in all the drawers and closets. He found a gun, and right away the idea came into his mind of doing something that was a little bigger than he was. He felt himself stronger than the other boys, and he thought of going out to let them see the gun he had. When he got outside, he met the other children and began to play with them, and then to frighten them he pointed the gun at them. A shot came from the pistol, which wounded one of the boys he was playing with. At the screams of the boy, all ran away and the wounded one was saved by a miracle. The boy, filled with fear, returned home, put the pistol away, and sat at the little table to study, hoping that his parents would not find out anything. But the parents had heard all about what happened before they even got home, and they gave the boy a lecture, feeling, however, a little responsible for what had happened and that luckily there were not serious consequences.

8. *Man, age 27.* A boy is sitting in front of a table with his head in his hands thinking. He is thinking of what he would like to be when he is big, and the violin that is before him is the subject of his thoughts. The violin has been in the house for many years, and the father plays it for amusement in his free hours after work and on Sundays. The boy is from a poor family and cannot have everything that he wishes. His father gave him the violin so that he could amuse himself. The boy is looking at the instrument, not because he thinks he can play it or learn it, but out of interest in an object that seems to him very beautiful, and he thinks that he would like to construct with his own hands something like it. The boy wants to become an artisan and make violins, guitars, mandolins, and other instruments of that kind. He is thinking about this and

he will tell his parents. They will do all they can so that the boy may be able to do what he wants, and they will send him to a school for artisans that he may learn his trade. The boy will continue his studies for many years and he will succeed in becoming a fine artisan and he will be able to assure himself of a modest living but a secure one.

9. *Woman, age 32.* A boy is looking at a violin and he is wondering what he can do in order to learn to play it. He knows that it takes money to learn and to go to school, but he hopes to succeed in learning by making his parents, and also some relatives, help him. His uncles love him very much, and they would be able to give him the little money he needs for the lessons. His parents, however, are not so happy that he wants to learn to play the violin, and they would rather that he work in the fields with them because they have need of his help. The boy has seen some players at the cinema and a great passion to play the violin too has come to him. His parents have bought him the violin, but they are not able to let him study because they have need of his work in the fields. The boy, in order not to be in disagreement with his parents, studies only in the hours when he is free from work instead of going out with the other boys to amuse himself. He will become a fine violinist, and he will go to play in a dance orchestra, but he will continue to live with his parents and even to help them with their work.

10. *Woman, age 36.* A little boy wants to learn to play the violin and spends all his free time after school trying to play it. But he is not able to because he does not know music nor the instrument, and thus he wastes time. His parents do not want their son to be a lazy boy. The first time the parents saw the boy with the violin they thought that he was just fooling around. But now they have seen that the boy even neglects school and does not do his homework in order to amuse himself with the violin, although he does not succeed in learning to play because he really has no will to do it. His parents have told him that there are two things—either he must set himself

to studying the violin seriously without wasting time, or he may amuse himself with it but only after he has finished his school work. The boy is now thinking on this but can't decide. The violin is only a whim for him, and he has no desire to learn to play. He will thus decide as his parents think. He will study what he is given to study at school, and then when he has time and inclination he will amuse himself with the violin.

RURAL KANSAS

1. *Man, age about 30.* It looks to me like a little kid's got to take violin lessons, and he seems to be pretty bored. It looks to me as though he's dreaming about some other kids outside—maybe there's a good ball game going on, I don't know. His mother probably wants him to be a great concert violinist someday, but he seems pretty bored. His mother probably gets her way; the little boy has to stay in and practice his violin lessons. |But in the end| he turns out to be a big league ball player.

2. *Woman, age about 30.* In a little village in Germany there lived a large family. There was not much opportunity for the children to go to school because there was a big family. This little boy had his head set on being a great musician. There was not much of a way to make any money, but he saved every penny he could get to later go to school and buy a violin. His brother and sisters all laughed at him for having a great ambition, but he said, "I'll show you." So he worked and slaved day after day. He studied at night. When he was old enough, he went away to college. It was not easy. But his family can all truthfully say they are proud; for today he is one of the nation's leading conductors.

3. *Man, age 35–40.* There's a young boy looking at his violin. He's probably been told he should practice his violin. He's thinking it over, trying to decide if he really wants to or not. I believe he would enjoy his violin if he would just pick it up and play it—but he can't quite make up his mind whether he wants to or not. He's thinking also that if he'd practice and

play real well, maybe some day he would become great and go out before large audiences and entertain the people, and get very rich. Pretty soon he's going to make up his mind to play the violin and become a great violinist.

4. *Woman, age 35–40.* This little boy has grown tired of practicing his violin lesson. He is thinking about doing something outside. While he is thinking about it, his mother probably tells him to get back to practicing so he probably does. As time goes by, he learns to play real well—perhaps gets so he enjoys it. He has a pet dog that always howls when he practices. As he grows older, he becomes quite accomplished, and plays in an orchestra.

5. *Man, age 35–40.* There's a boy thinking about his violin. He's probably disgusted because maybe he's supposed to practice with it. It looks like he's got a bad eye. I donno know much about that picture. (What happens?) I donno. He just ain't playing his violin.

Index